# LYSISTRATA AND OTHER PLAYS

## By ARISTOPHANES

A Digireads.com Book
Digireads.com Publishing

Lysistrata and Other Plays
By Aristophanes
ISBN 10: 1-4209-4758-3
ISBN 13: 978-1-4209-4758-8

Please visit *www.digireads.com*

# CONTENTS

4

# THE ACHARNIANS

## INTRODUCTION

This is the first of the series of three Comedies—'The Acharnians,' 'Peace' and 'Lysistrata'—produced at intervals of years, the sixth, tenth and twenty-first of the Peloponnesian War, and impressing on the Athenian people the miseries and disasters due to it and to the scoundrels who by their selfish and reckless policy had provoked it, the consequent ruin of industry and, above all, agriculture, and the urgency of asking Peace. In date it is the earliest play brought out by the author in his own name and his first work of serious importance. It was acted at the Lenaean Festival, in January, 426 B.C., and gained the first prize, Cratinus being second.

Its diatribes against the War and fierce criticism of the general policy of the War party so enraged Cleon that, as already mentioned, he endeavoured to ruin the author, who in 'The Knights' retorted by a direct and savage personal attack on the leader of the democracy.

The plot is of the simplest. Dicaeopolis, an Athenian citizen, but a native of Acharnae, one of the agricultural demes and one which had especially suffered in the Lacedaemonian invasions, sick and tired of the ill-success and miseries of the War, makes up his mind, if he fails to induce the people to adopt his policy of "peace at any price," to conclude a private and particular peace of his own to cover himself, his family, and his estate. The Athenians, momentarily elated by victory and over-persuaded by the demagogues of the day—Cleon and his henchmen, refuse to hear of such a thing as coming to terms. Accordingly Dicaeopolis dispatches an envoy to Sparta on his own account, who comes back presently with a selection of specimen treaties in his pocket. The old man tastes and tries, special terms are arranged, and the play concludes with a riotous and uproarious rustic feast in honour of the blessings of Peace and Plenty.

Incidentally excellent fun is poked at Euripides and his dramatic methods, which supply matter for so much witty badinage in several others of our author's pieces.

Other specially comic incidents are: the scene where the two young daughters of the famished Megarian are sold in the market at Athens as sucking-pigs—a scene in which the convenient similarity of the Greek words signifying a pig and the 'pudendum muliebre' respectively is utilized in a whole string of ingenious and suggestive 'double entendres' and ludicrous jokes; another where the Informer, or Market-Spy, is packed up in a crate as crockery and carried off home by the Boeotian buyer.

The drama takes its title from the Chorus, composed of old men of Acharnae.

## DRAMATIS PERSONAE

DICAEOPOLIS
HERALD
AMPHITHEUS
AMBASSADORS
PSEUDARTABAS
THEORUS
WIFE OF DICAEOPOLIS
DAUGHTER OF DICAEOPOLIS
EURIPIDES
CEPHISOPHON, *servant of Euripides*
LAMACHUS
ATTENDANT OF LAMACHUS
A MEGARIAN
MAIDENS, *daughters of the Megarian*
A BOEOTIAN
NICARCHUS
A HUSBANDMAN
A BRIDESMAID
AN INFORMER
MESSENGERS
CHORUS OF ACHARNIAN ELDERS

SCENE: *The Athenian Ecclesia on the Pnyx; afterwards Dicaeopolis' house in the country.*

# THE ACHARNIANS

DICAEOPOLIS.[1] [*alone.*] What cares have not gnawed at my heart and how few have been the pleasures in my life! Four, to be exact, while my troubles have been as countless as the grains of sand on the shore! Let me see! of what value to me have been these few pleasures? Ah! I remember that I was delighted in soul when Cleon had to disgorge those five talents;[2] I was in ecstasy and I love the Knights for this deed; 'it is an honour to Greece.'[3] But the day when I was impatiently awaiting a piece by Aeschylus,[4] what tragic despair it caused me when the herald called, "Theognis,[5] introduce your Chorus!" Just imagine how this blow struck straight at my heart! On the other hand, what joy Dexitheus caused me at the musical competition, when he played a Boeotian melody on the lyre! But this year by contrast! Oh! what deadly torture to hear Chaeris[6] perform the prelude in the Orthian mode![7]—Never, however, since I began to bathe, has the dust hurt my eyes as it does to-day. Still it is the day of assembly; all should be here at daybreak, and yet the Pnyx[8] is still deserted. They are gossiping in the marketplace, slipping hither and thither to avoid the vermilioned rope.[9] The Prytanes[10] even do not come; they will be late, but when they come they will push and fight each other for a seat in the front row. They will never trouble themselves with the question of peace. Oh! Athens! Athens! As for myself, I do not fail to come here before all the rest, and now, finding myself alone, I groan, yawn, stretch, break wind, and know not what to do; I make sketches in the dust, pull out my loose hairs, muse, think of my fields, long for peace, curse town life and regret my dear country home,[11] which never told me to 'buy fuel, vinegar or oil'; there the word 'buy,' which cuts me in two, was unknown; I harvested everything at will. Therefore I have come to the assembly fully prepared to bawl, interrupt and abuse the speakers, if they talk of anything but peace. But here come the Prytanes, and high time too, for it is midday! As I foretold, hah! is it not so? They are pushing and fighting for the front seats.

---

[1] A name invented by Aristophanes and signifying 'a just citizen.'

[2] Clean had received five talents from the islanders subject to Athens, on condition that he should get the tribute payable by them reduced; when informed of this transaction, the knights compelled him to return the money.

[3] A hemistich borrowed from Euripides' 'Telephus.'

[4] The tragedies of Aeschylus continued to be played even after the poet's death, which occurred in 436 B.C., ten years before the production of 'The Acharnians.'

[5] A tragic poet, whose pieces were so devoid of warmth and life that he was nicknamed [Greek excluded] 'snow.'

[6] A bad musician, frequently ridiculed by Aristophanes; he played both the lyre and the flute.

[7] A lively and elevated method.

[8] A hill near the Acropolis, where the Assemblies were held.

[9] Several means were used to force citizens to attend the assemblies; the shops were closed; circulation was only permitted in those streets which led to the Pnyx; finally, a rope covered with vermilion was drawn round those who dallied in the Agora (the market-place), and the late-comers, ear-marked by the imprint of the rope, were fined.

[10] Magistrates who, with the Archons and the Epistatae, shared the care of holding and directing the assemblies of the people; they were fifty in number.

[11] The Peloponnesian War had already, at the date of the representation of 'The Acharnians,' lasted five years, 431-426 B.C.; driven from their lands by the successive Lacedaemonian invasions, the people throughout the country had been compelled to seek shelter behind the walls of Athens.

HERALD. Move on up, move on, move on, to get within the consecrated area.[12]

AMPHITHEUS. Has anyone spoken yet?

HERALD. Who asks to speak?

AMPHITHEUS. I do.

HERALD. Your name?

AMPHITHEUS. Amphitheus.

HERALD. You are no man.[13]

AMPHITHEUS. No! I am an immortal! Amphitheus was the son of Ceres and Triptolemus; of him was born Celeus. Celeus wedded Phaenerete, my grandmother, whose son was Lucinus, and, being born of him I am an immortal; it is to me alone that the gods have entrusted the duty of treating with the Lacedaemonians. But, citizens, though I am immortal, I am dying of hunger; the Prytanes give me naught.[14]

A PRYTANIS. Guards!

AMPHITHEUS. Oh, Triptolemus and Ceres, do ye thus forsake your own blood?

DICAEOPOLIS. Prytanes, in expelling this citizen, you are offering an outrage to the Assembly. He only desired to secure peace for us and to sheathe the sword.

PRYTANIS. Sit down and keep silence!

DICAEOPOLIS. No, by Apollo, I will not, unless you are going to discuss the question of peace.

HERALD. The ambassadors, who are returned from the Court of the King!

DICAEOPOLIS. Of what King? I am sick of all those fine birds, the peacock ambassadors and their swagger.

HERALD. Silence!

DICAEOPOLIS. Oh! oh! by Ecbatana,[15] what a costume!

AN AMBASSADOR. During the archonship of Euthymenes, you sent us to the Great King on a salary of two drachmae per diem.

DICAEOPOLIS. Ah! those poor drachmae!

AMBASSADOR. We suffered horribly on the plains of the Cayster, sleeping under a tent, stretched deliciously on fine chariots, half dead with weariness.

DICAEOPOLIS. And I was very much at ease, lying on the straw along the battlements![16]

AMBASSADOR. Everywhere we were well received and forced to drink delicious wine out of golden or crystal flagons....

DICAEOPOLIS. Oh, city of Cranaus,[17] thy ambassadors are laughing at thee!

AMBASSADOR. For great feeders and heavy drinkers are alone esteemed as men by the barbarians.

DICAEOPOLIS. Just as here in Athens, we only esteem the most drunken debauchees.

AMBASSADOR. At the end of the fourth year we reached the King's Court, but he had left with his whole army to ease himself, and for the space of eight months he was

---

[12] Shortly before the meeting of the Assembly, a number of young pigs were immolated and a few drops of their blood were sprinkled on the seats of the Prytanes; this sacrifice was in honour of Ceres.

[13] The name, Amphitheus, contains the word [Greek excluded] 'god.'

[14] Amongst other duties, it was the office of the Prytanes to look after the wants of the poor.

[15] The summer residence of the Great King.

[16] Referring to the hardships he had endured garrisoning the walls of Athens during the Lacedaemonian invasions early in the War.

[17] Cranaus, the second king of Athens, the successor of Cecrops.

thus easing himself in the midst of the golden mountains.[18]

DICAEOPOLIS. And how long was he replacing his dress?

AMBASSADOR. The whole period of a full moon; after which he returned to his palace; then he entertained us and had us served with oxen roasted whole in an oven.

DICAEOPOLIS. Who ever saw an oxen baked in an oven? What a lie!

AMBASSADOR. On my honour, he also had us served with a bird three times as large as Cleonymus,[19] and called the Boaster.

DICAEOPOLIS. And do we give you two drachmae, that you should treat us to all this humbug?

AMBASSADOR. We are bringing to you Pseudartabas[20], the King's Eye.

DICAEOPOLIS. I would a crow might pluck out thine with his beak, you cursed ambassador!

HERALD. The King's Eye!

DICAEOPOLIS. Eh! Great Gods! Friend, with thy great eye, round like the hole through which the oarsman passes his sweep, you have the air of a galley doubling a cape to gain port.

AMBASSADOR. Come, Pseudartabas, give forth the message for the Athenians with which you were charged by the Great King.

PSEUDARTABAS. Jartaman exarx 'anapissonia satra.[21]

AMBASSADOR. Do you understand what he says?

DICAEOPOLIS. By Apollo, not I!

AMBASSADOR. [to THE PRYTANES.] He says that the Great King will send you gold. Come, utter the word 'gold' louder and more distinctly.

PSEUDARTABAS. Thou shalt not have gold, thou gaping-arsed Ionian.[22]

DICAEOPOLIS. Ah! may the gods forgive me, but that is clear enough!

AMBASSADOR. What does he say?

DICAEOPOLIS. That the Ionians are debauchees and idiots, if they expect to receive gold from the barbarians.

AMBASSADOR. Not so, he speaks of medimni[23] of gold.

DICAEOPOLIS. What medimni? Thou are but a great braggart; but get your way; I will find out the truth by myself. Come now, answer me clearly, if you do not wish me to dye your skin red. Will the Great King send us gold? [PSEUDARTABAS makes a negative sign.] Then our ambassadors are seeking to deceive us? [PSEUDARTABAS signs affirmatively.] These fellows make signs like any Greek; I am sure that they are nothing but Athenians. Oh! ho! I recognize one of these eunuchs; it is Clisthenes, the son of Sibyrtius.[24] Behold the effrontery of this shaven rump! How! great baboon, with such a beard do you seek to play the eunuch to us? And this other one? Is it not Straton?

HERALD. Silence! Let all be seated. The Senate invites the King's Eye to the

---

[18] Lucian, in his 'Hermotimus,' speaks of these golden mountains as an apocryphal land of wonders and prodigies.

[19] Cleonymus was an Athenian general of exceptionally tall stature; Aristophanes incessantly rallies him for his cowardice; he had cast away his buckler in a fight.

[20] A name borne by certain officials of the King of Persia. The actor of this part wore a mask, fitted with a single eye of great size.

[21] Jargon, no doubt meaningless in all languages.

[22] The Persians styled all Greeks 'Ionians' without distinction; here the Athenians are intended.

[23] A Greek measure, containing about six modii.

[24] Noted for his extreme ugliness and his obscenity. Aristophanes frequently holds him to scorn in his comedies.

Prytaneum.[25]

DICAEOPOLIS. Is this not sufficient to drive one to hang oneself? Here I stand chilled to the bone, whilst the doors of the Prytaneum fly wide open to lodge such rascals. But I will do something great and bold. Where is Amphitheus? Come and speak with me.

AMPHITHEUS. Here I am.

DICAEOPOLIS. Take these eight drachmae and go and conclude a truce with the Lacedaemonians for me, my wife and my children; I leave you free, my dear citizens, to send out embassies and to stand gaping in the air.

HERALD. Bring in Theorus, who has returned from the Court of Sitalces.[26]

THEORUS. I am here.

DICAEOPOLIS. Another humbug!

THEORUS. We should not have remained long in Thrace...

DICAEOPOLIS. Forsooth, no, if you had not been well paid.

THEORUS. ...if the country had not been covered with snow; the rivers were ice-bound at the time that Theognis[27] brought out his tragedy here; during the whole of that time I was holding my own with Sitalces, cup in hand; and, in truth, he adored you to such a degree, that he wrote on the walls, "How beautiful are the Athenians!" His son, to whom we gave the freedom of the city, burned with desire to come here and eat chitterlings at the feast of the Apaturia;[28] he prayed his father to come to the aid of his new country and Sitalces swore on his goblet that he would succour us with such a host that the Athenians would exclaim, "What a cloud of grasshoppers!"

DICAEOPOLIS. May I die if I believe a word of what you tell us! Excepting the grasshoppers, there is not a grain of truth in it all!

THEORUS. And he has sent you the most warlike soldiers of all Thrace.

DICAEOPOLIS. Now we shall begin to see clearly.

HERALD. Come hither, Thracians, whom Theorus brought.

DICAEOPOLIS. What plague have we here?

THEORUS. 'Tis the host of the Odomanti.[29]

DICAEOPOLIS. Of the Odomanti? Tell me what it means. Who has mutilated them like this?

THEORUS. If they are given a wage of two drachmae, they will put all Boeotia[30] to fire and sword.

DICAEOPOLIS. Two drachmae to those circumcised hounds! Groan aloud, ye people of rowers, bulwark of Athens! Ah! great gods! I am undone; these Odomanti are robbing me of my garlic![31] Will you give me back my garlic?

THEORUS. Oh! wretched man! do not go near them; they have eaten garlic[32].

DICAEOPOLIS. Prytanes, will you let me be treated in this manner, in my own country and by barbarians? But I oppose the discussion of paying a wage to the Thracians; I announce an omen; I have just felt a drop of rain.[33]

---

[25] Ambassadors were entertained there at the public expense.

[26] King of Thrace.

[27] The tragic poet.

[28] A feast lasting three days and celebrated during the month Pyanepsion (November). The Greek word contains the suggestion of fraud.

[29] A Thracian tribe from the right bank of the Strymon.

[30] The Boeotians were the allies of Sparta.

[31] Dicaeopolis had brought a clove of garlic with him to eat during the Assembly.

[32] Garlic was given to game-cocks, before setting them at each other, to give them pluck for the fight.

[33] At the lest unfavourable omen, the sitting of the Assembly was declared at an end.

HERALD. Let the Thracians withdraw and return the day after tomorrow; the Prytanes declare the sitting at an end.

DICAEOPOLIS. Ye gods, what garlic I have lost! But here comes Amphitheus returned from Lacedaemon. Welcome, Amphitheus.

AMPHITHEUS. No, there is no welcome for me and I fly as fast as I can, for I am pursued by the Acharnians.

DICAEOPOLIS. Why, what has happened?

AMPHITHEUS. I was hurrying to bring your treaty of truce, but some old dotards from Acharnae[34] got scent of the thing; they are veterans of Marathon, tough as oak or maple, of which they are made for sure—rough and ruthless. They all started a-crying: "Wretch! you are the bearer of a treaty, and the enemy has only just cut our vines!" Meanwhile they were gathering stones in their cloaks, so I fled and they ran after me shouting.

DICAEOPOLIS. Let 'em shout as much as they please! But *have* you brought me a treaty?

AMPHITHEUS. Most certainly, here are three samples to select from,[35] this one is five years old; take it and taste.

DICAEOPOLIS. Faugh!

AMPHITHEUS. Well?

DICAEOPOLIS. It does not please me; it smells of pitch and of the ships they are fitting out.[36]

AMPHITHEUS. Here is another, ten years old; taste it.

DICAEOPOLIS. It smells strongly of the delegates, who go around the towns to chide the allies for their slowness.[37]

AMPHITHEUS. This last is a truce of thirty years, both on sea and land.

DICAEOPOLIS. Oh! by Bacchus! what a bouquet! It has the aroma of nectar and ambrosia; this does not say to us, "Provision yourselves for three days." But it lisps the gentle numbers, "Go whither you will."[38] I accept it, ratify it, drink it at one draught and consign the Acharnians to limbo. Freed from the war and its ills, I shall keep the Dionysia[39] in the country.

AMPHITHEUS. And I shall run away, for I'm mortally afraid of the Acharnians.

CHORUS. This way all! Let us follow our man; we will demand him of everyone we meet; the public weal makes his seizure imperative. Ho, there! tell me which way the bearer of the truce has gone; he has escaped us, he has disappeared. Curse old age! When I was young, in the days when I followed Phayllus,[40] running with a sack of coals on my back, this wretch would not have eluded my pursuit, let him be as swift as he will; but now my limbs are stiff; old Lacratides[41] feels his legs are weighty and the traitor escapes me. No, no, let us follow him; old Acharnians like ourselves shall

---

[34] The deme of Acharnae was largely inhabited by charcoal-burners, who supplied the city with fuel.

[35] He presents them in the form of wines contained in three separate skins.

[36] Meaning, preparations for war.

[37] Meaning, securing allies for the continuance of the war.

[38] When Athens sent forth an army, the soldiers were usually ordered to assemble at some particular spot with provisions for three days.

[39] These feasts were also called the Anthesteria or Lenaea; the Lenaem was a temple to Bacchus, erected outside the city. They took place during the month Anthesterion (February).

[40] A celebrated athlete from Croton and a victor at Olympia; he was equally good as a runner and at the 'five exercises.'

[41] He had been Archon at the time of the battle of Marathon.

not be set at naught by a scoundrel, who has dared, great gods! to conclude a truce, when I wanted the war continued with double fury in order to avenge my ruined lands. No mercy for our foes until I have pierced their hearts like sharp reed, so that they dare never again ravage my vineyards. Come, let us seek the rascal; let us look everywhere, carrying our stones in our hands; let us hunt him from place to place until we trap him; I could never, never tire of the delight of stoning him.

DICAEOPOLIS. Peace! profane men![42]

CHORUS. Silence all! Friends, do you hear the sacred formula? Here is he, whom we seek! This way, all! Get out of his way, surely he comes to offer an oblation.

DICAEOPOLIS. Peace, profane men! Let the basket-bearer[43] come forward, and thou Xanthias, hold the phallus well upright.[44]

WIFE OF DICAEOPOLIS. Daughter, set down the basket and let us begin the sacrifice.

DAUGHTER OF DICAEOPOLIS. Mother, hand me the ladle, that I may spread the sauce on the cake.

DICAEOPOLIS. It is well! Oh, mighty Bacchus, it is with joy that, freed from military duty, I and all mine perform this solemn rite and offer thee this sacrifice; grant that I may keep the rural Dionysia without hindrance and that this truce of thirty years may be propitious for me.

WIFE OF DICAEOPOLIS. Come, my child, carry the basket gracefully and with a grave, demure face. Happy he, who shall be your possessor and embrace you so firmly at dawn,[45] that you belch wind like a weasel. Go forward, and have a care they don't snatch your jewels in the crowd.

DICAEOPOLIS. Xanthias, walk behind the basket-bearer and hold the phallus well erect; I will follow, singing the Phallic hymn; thou, wife, look on from the top of the terrace.[46] Forward! Oh, Phales,[47] companion of the orgies of Bacchus, night reveller, god of adultery, friend of young men, these past six[48] years I have not been able to invoke thee. With what joy I return to my farmstead, thanks to the truce I have concluded, freed from cares, from fighting and from Lamachuses![49] How much sweeter, oh Phales, oh, Phales, is it to surprise Thratta, the pretty wood-maid, Strymodorus' slave, stealing wood from Mount Phelleus, to catch her under the arms, to throw her on the ground and possess her, Oh, Phales, Phales! If thou wilt drink and bemuse thyself with me, we shall to-morrow consume some good dish in honour of the peace, and I will hang up my buckler over the smoking hearth.

CHORUS. It is he, he himself. Stone him, stone him, stone him, strike the wretch. All, all of you, pelt him, pelt him!

DICAEOPOLIS. What is this? By Heracles, you will smash my pot.[50]

CHORUS. It is you that we are stoning, you miserable scoundrel.

---

[42] A sacred formula, pronounced by the priest before offering the sacrifice.

[43] The maiden who carried the basket filled with fruits at the Dionysia in honour of Bacchus.

[44] The emblem of the fecundity of nature; it consisted of a representation, generally grotesquely exaggerated, of the male genital organs; the phallophori crowned with violets and ivy and their faces shaded with green foliage, sang improvised airs, call 'Phallics,' full of obscenity and suggestive 'double entendres.'

[45] The most propitious moment for Love's gambols, observes the scholiast.

[46] Married women did not join in the processions.

[47] The god of generation, worshipped in the form of a phallus.

[48] A remark which fixes the date of the production of 'The Acharnians,' viz. the sixth year of the Peloponnesian War, 426 B.C.

[49] Lamachus was an Athenian general, who figures later in this comedy.

[50] At the rural Dionysia a pot of kitchen vegetables was borne in the procession along with other emblems.

DICAEOPOLIS. And for what sin, Acharnian Elders, tell me that!

CHORUS. You ask that, you impudent rascal, traitor to your country; you alone amongst us all have concluded a truce, and you dare to look us in the face!

DICAEOPOLIS. But you do not know *why* I have treated for peace. Listen!

CHORUS. Listen to you? No, no, you are about to die, we will annihilate you with our stones.

DICAEOPOLIS. But first of all, listen. Stop, my friends.

CHORUS. I will hear nothing; do not address me; I hate you more than I do Cleon,[51] whom one day I shall flay to make sandals for the Knights. Listen to your long speeches, after you have treated with the Laconians? No, I will punish you.

DICAEOPOLIS. Friends, leave the Laconians out of debate and consider only whether I have not done well to conclude my truce.

CHORUS. Done well! when you have treated with a people who know neither gods, nor truth, nor faith.

DICAEOPOLIS. We attribute too much to the Laconians; as for myself, I know that they are not the cause of all our troubles.

CHORUS. Oh, indeed, rascal! You dare to use such language to me and then expect me to spare you!

DICAEOPOLIS. No, no, they are not the cause of all our troubles, and I who address you claim to be able to prove that they have much to complain of in us.

CHORUS. This passes endurance; my heart bounds with fury. Thus you dare to defend our enemies.

DICAEOPOLIS. Were my head on the block I would uphold what I say and rely on the approval of the people.

CHORUS. Comrades, let us hurl our stones and dye this fellow purple.

DICAEOPOLIS. What black fire-brand has inflamed your heart! You will not hear me? You really will not, Acharnians?

CHORUS. No, a thousand times, no.

DICAEOPOLIS. This is a hateful injustice.

CHORUS. May I die, if I listen.

DICAEOPOLIS. Nay, nay! have mercy, have mercy, Acharnians.

CHORUS. You shall die.

DICAEOPOLIS. Well, blood for blood! I will kill your dearest friend. I have here the hostages of Acharnae;[52] I shall disembowel them.

CHORUS. Acharnians, what means this threat? Has he got one of our children in his house? What gives him such audacity?

DICAEOPOLIS. Stone me, if it please you; I shall avenge myself on this. [*Shows a basket.*] Let us see whether you have any love for your coals.

CHORUS. Great Gods! this basket is our fellow-citizen. Stop, stop, in heaven's name!

DICAEOPOLIS. I shall dismember it despite your cries; I will listen to nothing.

CHORUS. How! will you kill this coal-basket, my beloved comrade?

DICAEOPOLIS. Just now, you would not listen to me.

CHORUS. Well, speak now, if you will; tell us, tell us you have a weakness for the Lacedaemonians. I consent to anything; never will I forsake this dear little basket.

DICAEOPOLIS. First, throw down your stones.

---

[51] Cleon the Demagogue was a currier originally by trade. He was the sworn foe and particular detestation of the Knights or aristocratic party generally.

[52] That is, the baskets of charcoal.

CHORUS. There! 'tis done. And you, do put away your sword.

DICAEOPOLIS. Let me see that no stones remain concealed in your cloaks.

CHORUS. They are all on the ground; see how we shake our garments. Come, no haggling, lay down your sword; we threw away everything while crossing from one side of the stage to the other.[53]

DICAEOPOLIS. What cries of anguish you would have uttered had these coals of Parnes[54] been dismembered, and yet it came very near it; had they perished, their death would have been due to the folly of their fellow-citizens. The poor basket was so frightened, look, it has shed a thick black dust over me, the same as a cuttle-fish does. What an irritable temper! You shout and throw stones, you will not hear my arguments—not even when I propose to speak in favour of the Lacedaemonians with my head on the block; and yet I cling to life.

CHORUS. Well then, bring out a block before your door, scoundrel, and let us hear the good grounds you can give us; I am curious to know them. Now mind, as you proposed yourself, place your head on the block and speak.

DICAEOPOLIS. Here is the block; and, though I am but a very sorry speaker, I wish nevertheless to talk freely of the Lacedaemonians and without the protection of my buckler. Yet I have many reasons for fear. I know our rustics; they are delighted if some braggart comes, and rightly or wrongly, loads both them and their city with praise and flattery; they do not see that such toad-eaters[55] are traitors, who sell them for gain. As for the old men, I know their weakness; they only seek to overwhelm the accused with their votes.[56] Nor have I forgotten how Cleon treated me because of my comedy last year;[57] he dragged me before the Senate and there he uttered endless slanders against me; 'twas a tempest of abuse, a deluge of lies. Through what a slough of mud he dragged me! I almost perished. Permit me, therefore, before I speak, to dress in the manner most likely to draw pity.

CHORUS. What evasions, subterfuges and delays! Hold! here is the sombre helmet of Pluto with its thick bristling plume; Hieronymus[58] lends it to you; then open Sisyphus'[59] bag of wiles; but hurry, hurry, pray, for discussion does not admit of delay.

DICAEOPOLIS. The time has come for me to manifest my courage, so I will go and seek Euripides. Ho! slave, slave!

SLAVE. Who's there?

DICAEOPOLIS. Is Euripides at home?

SLAVE. He is and he isn't; understand that, if you have wit for't.

DICAEOPOLIS. How? He is and he isn't![60]

SLAVE. Certainly, old man; busy gathering subtle fancies here and there, his mind is not

---

[53] The stage of the Greek theatre was much broader, and at the same time shallower, than in a modern playhouse.

[54] A mountain in Attica, in the neighbourhood of Acharnae.

[55] Orators in the pay of the enemy.

[56] Satire on the Athenians' addiction to law-suits.

[57] 'The Babylonians.' Cleon had denounced Aristophanes to the Senate for having scoffed at Athens before strangers, many of whom were present at the performance. The play is now lost.

[58] A tragic poet; we know next to nothing of him or his works.

[59] Son of Aeolus, renowned in fable for his robberies, and for the tortures to which he was put by Pluto. He was cunning enough to break loose out of hell, but Hermes brought him back again.

[60] This whole scene is directed at Euripides; Aristophanes ridicules the subtleties of his poetry and the trickeries of his staging, which, according to him, he only used to attract the less refined among his audience.

in the house, but he himself is; perched aloft, he is composing a tragedy.

DICAEOPOLIS. Oh, Euripides, you are indeed happy to have a slave so quick at repartee! Now, fellow, call your master.

SLAVE. Impossible!

DICAEOPOLIS. So much the worse. But I will not go. Come, let us knock at the door. Euripides, my little Euripides, my darling Euripides, listen; never had man greater right to your pity. It is Dicaeopolis of the Chollidan Deme who calls you. Do you hear?

EURIPIDES. I have no time to waste.

DICAEOPOLIS. Very well, have yourself wheeled out here.[61]

EURIPIDES. Impossible.

DICAEOPOLIS. Nevertheless...

EURIPIDES. Well, let them roll me out; as to coming down, I have not the time.

DICAEOPOLIS. Euripides....

EURIPIDES. What words strike my ear?

DICAEOPOLIS. You perch aloft to compose tragedies, when you might just as well do them on the ground. I am not astonished at your introducing cripples on the stage.[62] And why dress in these miserable tragic rags? I do not wonder that your heroes are beggars. But, Euripides, on my knees I beseech you, give me the tatters of some old piece; for I have to treat the Chorus to a long speech, and if I do it ill it is all over with me.

EURIPIDES. What rags do you prefer? Those in which I rigged out Aeneus[63] on the stage, that unhappy, miserable old man?

DICAEOPOLIS. No, I want those of some hero still more unfortunate.

EURIPIDES. Of Phoenix, the blind man?

DICAEOPOLIS. No, not of Phoenix, you have another hero more unfortunate than him.

EURIPIDES. Now, what tatters *does* he want? Do you mean those of the beggar Philoctetes?

DICAEOPOLIS. No, of another far more the mendicant.

EURIPIDES. Is it the filthy dress of the lame fellow, Bellerophon?

DICAEOPOLIS. No, 'tis not Bellerophon; he, whom I mean, was not only lame and a beggar, but boastful and a fine speaker.

EURIPIDES. Ah! I know, it is Telephus, the Mysian.

DICAEOPOLIS. Yes, Telephus. Give me his rags, I beg of you.

EURIPIDES. Slave! give him Telephus' tatters; they are on top of the rags of Thyestes and mixed with those of Ino.

SLAVE. Catch hold! here they are.

DICAEOPOLIS. Oh! Zeus, whose eye pierces everywhere and embraces all, permit me to assume the most wretched dress on earth. Euripides, cap your kindness by giving me the little Mysian hat, that goes so well with these tatters. I must to-day have the

---

[61] "Wheeled out"—that is, by means of a mechanical contrivance of the Greek stage, by which an interior was shown, the set scene with performers, etc., all complete, being in some way, which cannot be clearly made out from the descriptions, swung out or wheeled out on to the main stage.

[62] Having been lamed, it is of course implied, by tumbling from the lofty apparatus on which the Author sat perched to write his tragedies.

[63] Euripides delighted, or was supposed by his critic Aristophanes to delight, in the representation of misery and wretchedness on the stage. 'Aeneus,' 'Phoenix,' 'Philoctetes,' 'Bellerophon,' 'Telephus,' 'Ino' are titles of six tragedies of his in this genre of which fragments are extant.

look of a beggar; "be what I am, but not appear to be";[64] the audience will know well who I am, but the Chorus will be fools enough not to, and I shall dupe 'em with my subtle phrases.

EURIPIDES. I will give you the hat; I love the clever tricks of an ingenious brain like yours.

DICAEOPOLIS. Rest happy, and may it befall Telephus as I wish. Ah! I already feel myself filled with quibbles. But I must have a beggar's staff.

EURIPIDES. Here you are, and now get you gone from this porch.

DICAEOPOLIS. Oh, my soul! You see how you are driven from this house, when I still need so many accessories. But let us be pressing, obstinate, importunate. Euripides, give me a little basket with a lamp alight inside.

EURIPIDES. Whatever do you want such a thing as that for?

DICAEOPOLIS. I do not need it, but I want it all the same.

EURIPIDES. You importune me; get you gone!

DICAEOPOLIS. Alas! may the gods grant you a destiny as brilliant as your mother's.[65]

EURIPIDES. Leave me in peace.

DICAEOPOLIS. Oh, just a little broken cup.

EURIPIDES. Take it and go and hang yourself. What a tiresome fellow!

DICAEOPOLIS. Ah! you do not know all the pain you cause me. Dear, good Euripides, nothing beyond a small pipkin stoppered with a sponge.

EURIPIDES. Miserable man! You are robbing me of an entire tragedy.[66] Here, take it and be off.

DICAEOPOLIS. I am going, but, great gods! I need one thing more; unless I have it, I am a dead man. Hearken, my little Euripides, only give me this and I go, never to return. For pity's sake, do give me a few small herbs for my basket.

EURIPIDES. You wish to ruin me then. Here, take what you want; but it is all over with my pieces!

DICAEOPOLIS. I won't ask another thing; I'm going. I am too importunate and forget that I rouse against me the hate of kings.—Ah! wretch that I am! I am lost! I have forgotten one thing, without which all the rest is as nothing. Euripides, my excellent Euripides, my dear little Euripides, may I die if I ask you again for the smallest present; only one, the last, absolutely the last; give me some of the chervil your mother left you in her will.

EURIPIDES. Insolent hound! Slave, lock the door!

DICAEOPOLIS. Oh, my soul! I must go away without the chervil. Art thou sensible of the dangerous battle we are about to engage upon in defending the Lacedaemonians? Courage, my soul, we must plunge into the midst of it. Dost thou hesitate and art thou fully steeped in Euripides? That's right! do not falter, my poor heart, and let us risk our head to say what we hold for truth. Courage and boldly to the front. I wonder I am so brave.

CHORUS. What do you purport doing? what are you going to say? What an impudent fellow! what a brazen heart! to dare to stake his head and uphold an opinion contrary to that of us all! And he does not tremble to face this peril. Come, it is you who desired it, speak!

---

[64] Line borrowed from Euripides. A great number of verses are similarly parodied in this scene.

[65] Report said that Euripides' mother had sold vegetables on the market.

[66] Aristophanes means, of course, to imply that the whole talent of Euripides lay in these petty details of stage property.

DICAEOPOLIS. Spectators, be not angered if, although I am a beggar, I dare in a Comedy to speak before the people of Athens of the public weal; Comedy too can sometimes discern what is right. I shall not please, but I shall say what is true. Besides, Cleon shall not be able to accuse me of attacking Athens before strangers;[67] we are by ourselves at the festival of the Lenaea; the period when our allies send us their tribute and their soldiers is not yet. Here is only the pure wheat without chaff; as to the resident strangers settled among us, they and the citizens are one, like the straw and the ear.

I detest the Lacedaemonians with all my heart, and may Posidon, the god of Taenarus,[68] cause an earthquake and overturn their dwellings! My vines also have been cut. But come (there are only friends who hear me), why accuse the Laconians of all our woes? Some men (I do not say the city, note particularly that I do not say the city), some wretches, lost in vices, bereft of honour, who were not even citizens of good stamp, but strangers, have accused the Megarians of introducing their produce fraudulently, and not a cucumber, a leveret, a sucking pig, a clove of garlic, a lump of salt was seen without its being said, "Halloa! these come from Megara," and their being instantly confiscated. Thus far the evil was not serious and we were the only sufferers. But now some young drunkards go to Megara and carry off the courtesan Simaetha; the Megarians, hurt to the quick, run off in turn with two harlots of the house of Aspasia; and so for three gay women Greece is set ablaze. Then Pericles, aflame with ire on his Olympian height, let loose the lightning, caused the thunder to roll, upset Greece and passed an edict, which ran like the song, "That the Megarians be banished both from our land and from our markets and from the sea and from the continent."[69] Meanwhile the Megarians, who were beginning to die of hunger, begged the Lacedaemonians to bring about the abolition of the decree, of which those harlots were the cause; several times we refused their demand; and from that time there was horrible clatter of arms everywhere. You will say that Sparta was wrong, but what should she have done? Answer that. Suppose that a Lacedaemonian had seized a little Seriphian[70] dog on any pretext and had sold it, would you have endured it quietly? Far from it, you would at once have sent three hundred vessels to sea, and what an uproar there would have been through all the city! there 'tis a band of noisy soldiery, here a brawl about the election of a Trierarch; elsewhere pay is being distributed, the Pallas figure-heads are being regilded, crowds are surging under the market porticos, encumbered with wheat that is being measured, wine-skins, oar-leathers, garlic, olives, onions in nets; everywhere are chaplets, sprats, flute-girls, black eyes; in the arsenal bolts are being noisily driven home, sweeps are being made and fitted with leathers; we hear nothing but the sound of whistles, of flutes and fifes to encourage the work-folk. That is what you assuredly would have done, and would not Telephus have done the same? So I come to my general conclusion; we have no common sense.

FIRST SEMI-CHORUS. Oh! wretch! oh! infamous man! You are naught but a beggar

---

[67] 'The Babylonians' had been produced at a time of year when Athens was crowded with strangers; 'The Acharnians,' on the contrary, was played in December.

[68] Sparta had been menaced with an earthquake in 427 B.C. Posidon was 'The Earthshaker,' god of earthquakes, as well as of the sea.

[69] A song by Timocreon the Rhodian, the words of which were practically identical with Pericles' decree.

[70] A small and insignificant island, one of the Cyclades, allied with the Athenians, like months of these islands previous to and during the first part of the Peloponnesian War.

and yet you dare to talk to us like this! you insult their worships the informers!

SECOND SEMI-CHORUS. By Posidon! he speaks the truth; he has not lied in a single detail.

FIRST SEMI-CHORUS. But though it be true, need he say it? But you'll have no great cause to be proud of your insolence!

SECOND SEMI-CHORUS. Where are you running to? Don't you move; if you strike this man, I shall be at you.

FIRST SEMI-CHORUS. Lamachus, whose glance flashes lightning, whose plume petrifies thy foes, help! Oh! Lamachus, my friend, the hero of my tribe and all of you, both officers and soldiers, defenders of our walls, come to my aid; else is it all over with me!

LAMACHUS. Whence comes this cry of battle? where must I bring my aid? where must I sow dread? who wants me to uncase my dreadful Gorgon's head?[71]

DICAEOPOLIS. Oh, Lamachus, great hero! Your plumes and your cohorts terrify me.

CHORUS. This man, Lamachus, incessantly abuses Athens.

LAMACHUS. You are but a mendicant and you dare to use language of this sort?

DICAEOPOLIS. Oh, brave Lamachus, forgive a beggar who speaks at hazard.

LAMACHUS. But what have you said? Let us hear.

DICAEOPOLIS. I know nothing about it; the sight of weapons makes me dizzy. Oh! I adjure you, take that fearful Gorgon somewhat farther away.

LAMACHUS. There.

DICAEOPOLIS. Now place it face downwards on the ground.

LAMACHUS. It is done.

DICAEOPOLIS. Give me a plume out of your helmet.

LAMACHUS. Here is a feather.

DICAEOPOLIS. And hold my head while I vomit; the plumes have turned my stomach.

LAMACHUS. Hah! what are you proposing to do? do you want to make yourself vomit with this feather?

DICAEOPOLIS. Is it a feather? what bird's? a braggart's?

LAMACHUS. Ah! ah! I will rip you open.

DICAEOPOLIS. No, no, Lamachus! Violence is out of place here! But as you are so strong, why did you not circumcise me? You have all the tools you want for the operation there.

LAMACHUS. A beggar dares thus address a general!

DICAEOPOLIS. How? Am I a beggar?

LAMACHUS. What are you then?

DICAEOPOLIS. Who am I? A good citizen, not ambitious; a soldier, who has fought well since the outbreak of the war, whereas you are but a vile mercenary.

LAMACHUS. They elected me...

DICAEOPOLIS. Yes, three cuckoos did![72] If I have concluded peace, 'twas disgust that drove me; for I see men with hoary heads in the ranks and young fellows of your age shirking service. Some are in Thrace getting an allowance of three drachmae, such fellows as Tisamenophoenippus and Panurgipparchides. The others are with Chares or in Chaonia, men like Geretotheodorus and Diomialazon; there are some of the

[71] A figure of Medusa's head, forming the centre of Lamachus' shield.
[72] Indicates the character of his election, which was arranged, so Aristophanes implies, by his partisans.

same kidney, too, at Camarina and at Gela,[73] the laughing-stock of all and sundry.

LAMACHUS. They were elected.

DICAEOPOLIS. And why do you always receive your pay, when none of these others ever gets any? Speak, Marilades, you have grey hair; well then, have you ever been entrusted with a mission? See! he shakes his head. Yet he is an active as well as a prudent man. And you, Dracyllus, Euphorides or Prinides, have you knowledge of Ecbatana or Chaonia? You say no, do you not? Such offices are good for the son of Caesyra[74] and Lamachus, who, but yesterday ruined with debt, never pay their shot, and whom all their friends avoid as foot passengers dodge the folks who empty their slops out of window.

LAMACHUS. Oh! in freedom's name! are such exaggerations to be borne?

DICAEOPOLIS. Lamachus is well content; no doubt he is well paid, you know.

LAMACHUS. But I propose always to war with the Peloponnesians, both at sea, on land and everywhere to make them tremble, and trounce them soundly.

DICAEOPOLIS. For my own part, I make proclamation to all Peloponnesians, Megarians and Boeotians, that to them my markets are open; but I debar Lamachus from entering them.

CHORUS. Convinced by this man's speech, the folk have changed their view and approve him for having concluded peace. But let us prepare for the recital of the parabasis.[75]

Never since our poet presented Comedies, has he praised himself upon the stage; but, having been slandered by his enemies amongst the volatile Athenians, accused of scoffing at his country and of insulting the people, to-day he wishes to reply and regain for himself the inconstant Athenians. He maintains that he has done much that is good for you; if you no longer allow yourselves to be too much hoodwinked by strangers or seduced by flattery, if in politics you are no longer the ninnies you once were, it is thanks to him. Formerly, when delegates from other cities wanted to deceive you, they had but to style you, "the people crowned with violets," and at the word "violets" you at once sat erect on the tips of your bums. Or if, to tickle your vanity, someone spoke of "rich and sleek Athens," in return for that "sleekness" he would get all, because he spoke of you as he would have of anchovies in oil. In cautioning you against such wiles, the poet has done you great service as well as in forcing you to understand what is really the democratic principle. Thus, the strangers, who came to pay their tributes, wanted to see this great poet, who had dared to speak the truth to Athens. And so far has the fame of his boldness reached that one day the Great King, when questioning the Lacedaemonian delegates, first asked them which of the two rival cities was the superior at sea, and then immediately demanded at which it was that the comic poet directed his biting satire. "Happy that city," he added, "if it listens to his counsel; it will grow in power, and its victory is assured." This is why the Lacedaemonians offer you peace, if you will cede them Aegina; not that they care for the isle, but they wish to rob you of your

---

[73] Town in Sicily. There is a pun on the name Gela and 'ridiculous' which it is impossible to keep in English. Apparently the Athenians had sent embassies to all parts of the Greek world to arrange treaties of alliance in view of the struggle with the Lacedaemonians; but only young debauchees of aristocratic connections had been chosen as envoys.

[74] A contemporary orator apparently, otherwise unknown.

[75] The 'parabasis' in the Old Comedy was a sort of address or topical harangue addressed directly by the poet, speaking by the Chorus, to the audience. It was nearly always political in bearing, and the subject of the particular piece was for the time being set aside altogether.

poet.[76] As for you, never lose him, who will always fight for the cause of justice in his Comedies; he promises you that his precepts will lead you to happiness, though he uses neither flattery, nor bribery, nor intrigue, nor deceit; instead of loading you with praise, he will point you to the better way. I scoff at Cleon's tricks and plotting; honesty and justice shall fight my cause; never will you find me a political poltroon, a prostitute to the highest bidder.

I invoke thee, Acharnian Muse, fierce and fell as the devouring fire; sudden as the spark that bursts from the crackling oaken coal when roused by the quickening fan to fry little fishes, while others knead the dough or whip the sharp Thasian pickle with rapid hand, so break forth, my Muse, and inspire thy tribesmen with rough, vigorous, stirring strains.

We others, now old men and heavy with years, we reproach the city; so many are the victories we have gained for the Athenian fleets that we well deserve to be cared for in our declining life; yet far from this, we are ill-used, harassed with law-suits, delivered over to the scorn of stripling orators. Our minds and bodies being ravaged with age, Posidon should protect us, yet we have no other support than a staff. When standing before the judge, we can scarcely stammer forth the fewest words, and of justice we see but its barest shadow, whereas the accuser, desirous of conciliating the younger men, overwhelms us with his ready rhetoric; he drags us before the judge, presses us with questions, lays traps for us; the onslaught troubles, upsets and ruins poor old Tithonus, who, crushed with age, stands tongue-tied; sentenced to a fine,[77] he weeps, he sobs and says to his friend, "This fine robs me of the last trifle that was to have bought my coffin."

Is this not a scandal? What! the clepsydra[78] is to kill the white-haired veteran, who, in fierce fighting, has so oft covered himself with glorious sweat, whose valour at Marathon saved the country! 'Twas we who pursued on the field of Marathon, whereas now 'tis wretches who pursue us to the death and crush us! What would Marpsias reply to this?[79] What an injustice that a man, bent with age like Thucydides, should be brow-beaten by this braggart advocate, Cephisodemus,[80] who is as savage as the Scythian desert he was born in! Is it not to convict him from the outset? I wept tears of pity when I saw an Archer[81] maltreat this old man, who, by Ceres, when he was young and the true Thucydides, would not have permitted an insult from Ceres herself! At that date he would have floored ten orators, he would have terrified three thousand Archers with his shouts; he would have pierced the whole line of the enemy with his shafts. Ah! but if you will not leave the aged in peace, decree that the advocates be matched; thus the old man will only be confronted with a toothless grey-beard, the young will fight with the braggart, the ignoble with the son of Clinias;[82] make a law that in the future, the old man can only be summoned and convicted at the courts by the aged and the young man by the youth.

DICAEOPOLIS. These are the confines of my market-place. All Peloponnesians,

---

[76] It will be remembered that Aristophanes owned land in Aegina.

[77] Everything was made the object of a law-suit in Athens. The old soldiers, inexpert at speaking, often lost the day.

[78] A water-clock used to limit the length of speeches in the courts.

[79] A braggart speaker, fiery and pugnacious.

[80] Cephisodemus was an Athenian, but through his mother possessed Scythian blood.

[81] The city of Athens was policed by Scythian archers.

[82] Alcibiades.

Megarians, Boeotians, have the right to come and trade here, provided they sell their wares to me and not to Lamachus. As market-inspectors I appoint these three whips of Leprean[83] leather, chosen by lot. Warned away are all informers and all men of Phasis.[84] They are bringing me the pillar on which the treaty is inscribed[85] and I shall erect it in the centre of the market, well in sight of all.

A MEGARIAN. Hail! market of Athens, beloved of Megarians. Let Zeus, the patron of friendship, witness, I regretted you as a mother mourns her son. Come, poor little daughters of an unfortunate father, try to find something to eat; listen to me with the full heed of an empty belly. Which would you prefer? To be sold or to cry with hunger?

DAUGHTERS. To be sold, to be sold!

MEGARIAN. That is my opinion too. But who would make so sorry a deal as to buy you? Ah! I recall me a Megarian trick; I am going to disguise you as little porkers, that I am offering for sale. Fit your hands with these hoofs and take care to appear the issue of a sow of good breed, for, if I am forced to take you back to the house, by Hermes! you will suffer cruelly of hunger! Then fix on these snouts and cram yourselves into this sack. Forget not to grunt and to say wee-wee like the little pigs that are sacrificed in the Mysteries. I must summon Dicaeopolis. Where is be? Dicaeopolis, do you want to buy some nice little porkers?

DICAEOPOLIS. Who are you? a Megarian?

MEGARIAN. I have come to your market.

DICAEOPOLIS. Well, how are things at Megara?[86]

MEGARIAN. We are crying with hunger at our firesides.

DICAEOPOLIS. The fireside is jolly enough with a piper. But what else is doing at Megara, eh?

MEGARIAN. What else? When I left for the market, the authorities were taking steps to let us die in the quickest manner.

DICAEOPOLIS. That is the best way to get you out of all your troubles.

MEGARIAN. True.

DICAEOPOLIS. What other news of Megara? What is wheat selling at?

MEGARIAN. With us it is valued as highly as the very gods in heaven!

DICAEOPOLIS. Is it salt that you are bringing?

MEGARIAN. Are you not holding back the salt?

DICAEOPOLIS. 'Tis garlic then?

MEGARIAN. What! garlic! do you not at every raid grub up the ground with your pikes to pull out every single head?

DICAEOPOLIS. What *do* you bring then?

MEGARIAN. Little sows, like those they immolate at the Mysteries.

DICAEOPOLIS. Ah! very well, show me them.

MEGARIAN. They are very fine; feel their weight. See! how fat and fine.

DICAEOPOLIS. But what is this?

MEGARIAN. A *sow*, for a certainty.[87]

---

[83] The leather market was held in Lepros, outside the city.
[84] Meaning an informer ([from the Greek] 'to denounce').
[85] According to the Athenian custom.
[86] Megara was allied to Sparta and suffered during the war more than any other city because of its proximity to Athens.

DICAEOPOLIS. You say a sow! Of what country, then?

MEGARIAN. From Megara. What! is it not a sow then?

DICAEOPOLIS. No, I don't believe it is.

MEGARIAN. This is too much! what an incredulous man! He says 'tis not a sow; but we will stake, an you will, a measure of salt ground up with thyme, that in good Greek this is called a sow and nothing else.

DICAEOPOLIS. But a sow of the human kind.

MEGARIAN. Without question, by Diocles! of my own breed! Well! What think you? will you hear them squeal?

DICAEOPOLIS. Well, yes, I' faith, I will.

MEGARIAN. Cry quickly, wee sowlet; squeak up, hussy, or by Hermes! I take you back to the house.

GIRL. Wee-wee, wee-wee!

MEGARIAN. Is that a little sow, or not?

DICAEOPOLIS. Yes, it seems so; but let it grow up, and it will be a fine fat bitch.

MEGARIAN. In five years it will be just like its mother.

DICAEOPOLIS. But it cannot be sacrificed.

MEGARIAN. And why not?

DICAEOPOLIS. It has no tail.[88]

MEGARIAN. Because it is quite young, but in good time it will have a big one, thick and red.

DICAEOPOLIS. The two are as like as two peas.

MEGARIAN. They are born of the same father and mother; let them be fattened, let them grow their bristles, and they will be the finest sows you can offer to Aphrodite.

DICAEOPOLIS. But sows are not immolated to Aphrodite.

MEGARIAN. Not sows to Aphrodite! Why, 'tis the only goddess to whom they are offered! the flesh of my sows will be excellent on the spit.

DICAEOPOLIS. Can they eat alone? They no longer need their mother!

MEGARIAN. Certainly not, nor their father.

DICAEOPOLIS. What do they like most?

MEGARIAN. Whatever is given them; but ask for yourself.

DICAEOPOLIS. Speak! little sow.

DAUGHTER. Wee-wee, wee-wee!

DICAEOPOLIS. Can you eat chick-pease?

DAUGHTER. Wee-wee, wee-wee, wee-wee!

DICAEOPOLIS. And Attic figs?

DAUGHTER. Wee-wee, wee-wee!

DICAEOPOLIS. What sharp squeaks at the name of figs. Come, let some figs be brought for these little pigs. Will they eat them? Goodness! how they munch them, what a grinding of teeth, mighty Heracles! I believe those pigs hail from the land of the Voracians. But surely 'tis impossible they have bolted all the figs!

MEGARIAN. Yes, certainly, bar this one that I took from them.

DICAEOPOLIS. Ah! what funny creatures! For what sum will you sell them?

MEGARIAN. I will give you one for a bunch of garlic, and the other, if you like, for a

---

[87] Throughout this whole scene there is an obscene play upon the word [Greek excluded], which means in Greek both 'sow' and 'a woman's organs of generation.'

[88] Sacrificial victims were bound to be perfect in every part; an animal, therefore, without a tail could not be offered.

quart measure of salt.

DICAEOPOLIS. I buy them of you. Wait for me here.

MEGARIAN. The deal is done. Hermes, god of good traders, grant I may sell both my wife and my mother in the same way!

AN INFORMER. Hi! fellow, what countryman are you?

MEGARIAN. I am a pig-merchant from Megara.

INFORMER. I shall denounce both your pigs and yourself as public enemies.

MEGARIAN. Ah! here our troubles begin afresh!

INFORMER. Let go that sack. I will punish your Megarian lingo![89]

MEGARIAN. Dicaeopolis, Dicaeopolis, they want to denounce me.

DICAEOPOLIS. Who dares do this thing? Inspectors, drive out the informers. Ah! you offer to enlighten us without a lamp![90]

INFORMER. What! I may not denounce our enemies?

DICAEOPOLIS. Have a care for yourself, if you don't go off pretty quick to denounce elsewhere.

MEGARIAN. What a plague to Athens!

DICAEOPOLIS. Be reassured, Megarian. Here is the price for your two swine, the garlic and the salt. Farewell and much happiness!

MEGARIAN. Ah! we never have that amongst us.

DICAEOPOLIS. Well! may the inopportune wish apply to myself.

MEGARIAN. Farewell, dear little sows, and seek, far from your father, to munch your bread with salt, if they give you any.

CHORUS. Here is a man truly happy. See how everything succeeds to his wish. Peacefully seated in his market, he will earn his living; woe to Ctesias,[91] and all other informers who dare to enter there! You will not be cheated as to the value of wares, you will not again see Prepis[92] wiping his foul rump, nor will Cleonymus[93] jostle you; you will take your walks, clothed in a fine tunic, without meeting Hyperbolus[94] and his unceasing quibblings, without being accosted on the public place by any importunate fellow, neither by Cratinus,[95] shaven in the fashion of the debauchees, nor by this musician, who plagues us with his silly improvisations, Artemo, with his arm-pits stinking as foul as a goat, like his father before him. You will not be the butt of the villainous Pauson's[96] jeers, nor of Lysistratus,[97] the disgrace of the Cholargian deme, who is the incarnation of all the vices, and endures cold and hunger more than thirty days in the month.

A BOEOTIAN. By Heracles! my shoulder is quite black and blue. Ismenias, put the penny-royal down there very gently, and all of you, musicians from Thebes, pipe with your bone flutes into a dog's rump.[98]

DICAEOPOLIS. Enough, enough, get you gone. Rascally hornets, away with you!

---

[89] The Megarians used the Doric dialect.

[90] A play upon the word [Greek excluded] which both means 'to light' and 'to denounce.'

[91] An informer (sycophant), otherwise unknown.

[92] A debauchee of vile habits; a pathic.

[93] Mentioned above; he was as proud as he was cowardly.

[94] An Athenian general, quarrelsome and litigious, and an Informer into the bargain.

[95] A comic poet of vile habits.

[96] A painter.

[97] A debauchee, a gambler, and always in extreme poverty.

[98] This kind of flute had a bellows, made of dog-skin, much like the bagpipes of to-day.

Whence has sprung this accursed swarm of Charis[99] fellows which comes assailing my door?

BOEOTIAN. Ah! by Iolas![100] Drive them off, my dear host, you will please me immensely; all the way from Thebes, they were there piping behind me and have completely stripped my penny-royal of its blossom. But will you buy anything of me, some chickens or some locusts?

DICAEOPOLIS. Ah! good day, Boeotian, eater of good round loaves.[101] What do you bring?

BOEOTIAN. All that is good in Boeotia, marjoram, penny-royal, rush-mats, lamp-wicks, ducks, jays, woodcocks, water-fowl, wrens, divers.

DICAEOPOLIS. 'Tis a very hail of birds that beats down on my market.

BOEOTIAN. I also bring geese, hares, foxes, moles, hedgehogs, cats, lyres, martins, otters and eels from the Copaic lake.[102]

DICAEOPOLIS. Ah! my friend, you, who bring me the most delicious of fish, let me salute your eels.

BOEOTIAN. Come, thou, the eldest of my fifty Copaic virgins, come and complete the joy of our host.

DICAEOPOLIS. Oh! my well-beloved, thou object of my long regrets, thou art here at last then, thou, after whom the comic poets sigh, thou, who art dear to Morychus.[103] Slaves, hither with the stove and the bellows. Look at this charming eel, that returns to us after six long years of absence.[104] Salute it, my children; as for myself, I will supply coal to do honour to the stranger. Take it into my house; death itself could not separate me from her, if cooked with beet leaves.

BOEOTIAN. And what will you give me in return?

DICAEOPOLIS. It will pay for your market dues. And as to the rest, what do you wish to sell me?

BOEOTIAN. Why, everything.

DICAEOPOLIS. On what terms? For ready-money or in wares from these parts?

BOEOTIAN. I would take some Athenian produce, that we have not got in Boeotia.

DICAEOPOLIS. Phaleric anchovies, pottery?

BOEOTIAN. Anchovies, pottery? But these we have. I want produce that is wanting with us and that is plentiful here.

DICAEOPOLIS. Ah! I have the very thing; take away an Informer, packed up carefully as crockery-ware.

BOEOTIAN. By the twin gods! I should earn big money, if I took one; I would exhibit him as an ape full of spite.

DICAEOPOLIS. Hah! here we have Nicarchus,[105] who comes to denounce you.

BOEOTIAN. How small he is!

DICAEOPOLIS. But in his case the whole is one mass of ill-nature.

NICARCHUS. Whose are these goods?

DICAEOPOLIS. Mine; they come from Boeotia, I call Zeus to witness.

---

[99] A flute-player, mentioned above.

[100] A hero, much honoured in Thebes; nephew of Heracles.

[101] A form of bread peculiar to Boeotia.

[102] A lake in Boeotia.

[103] He was the Lucullus of Athens.

[104] This again fixes the date of the presentation of 'The Acharnians' to 436 B.C., the sixth year of the War, since the beginning of which Boeotia had been closed to the Athenians.

[105] An informer.

NICARCHUS. I denounce them as coming from an enemy's country.

BOEOTIAN. What! you declare war against birds?

NICARCHUS. And I am going to denounce you too.

BOEOTIAN. What harm have I done you?

NICARCHUS. I will say it for the benefit of those that listen; you introduce lamp-wicks from an enemy's country.

DICAEOPOLIS. Then you go as far as denouncing a wick.

NICARCHUS. It needs but one to set an arsenal afire.

DICAEOPOLIS. A wick set an arsenal ablaze! But how, great gods?

NICARCHUS. Should a Boeotian attach it to an insect's wing, and, taking advantage of a violent north wind, throw it by means of a tube into the arsenal and the fire once get hold of the vessels, everything would soon be devoured by the flames.

DICAEOPOLIS. Ah! wretch! an insect and a wick devour everything! [*He strikes him.*]

NICARCHUS. [*to the Chorus.*] You will bear witness, that he mishandles me.

DICAEOPOLIS. Shut his mouth. Give me some hay; I am going to pack him up like a vase, that he may not get broken on the road.

CHORUS. Pack up your goods carefully, friend; that the stranger may not break it when taking it away.

DICAEOPOLIS. I shall take great care with it, for one would say he is cracked already; he rings with a false note, which the gods abhor.

CHORUS. But what will be done with him?

DICAEOPOLIS. This is a vase good for all purposes; it will be used as a vessel for holding all foul things, a mortar for pounding together law-suits, a lamp for spying upon accounts, and as a cup for the mixing up and poisoning of everything.

CHORUS. None could ever trust a vessel for domestic use that has such a ring about it.

DICAEOPOLIS. Oh! it is strong, my friend, and will never get broken, if care is taken to hang it head downwards.

CHORUS. There! it is well packed now!

BOEOTIAN. Marry, I will proceed to carry off my bundle.

CHORUS. Farewell, worthiest of strangers, take this informer, good for anything, and fling him where you like.

DICAEOPOLIS. Bah! this rogue has given me enough trouble to pack! Here! Boeotian, pick up your pottery.

BOEOTIAN. Stoop, Ismenias, that I may put it on your shoulder, and be very careful with it.

DICAEOPOLIS. You carry nothing worth having; however, take it, for you will profit by your bargain; the Informers will bring you luck.

A SERVANT OF LAMACHUS. Dicaeopolis!

DICAEOPOLIS. What do you want crying this gait?

SERVANT. Lamachus wants to keep the Feast of Cups,[106] and I come by his order to bid you one drachma for some thrushes and three more for a Copaic eel.

DICAEOPOLIS. And who is this Lamachus, who demands an eel?

SERVANT. 'Tis the terrible, indefatigable Lamachus, who is always brandishing his fearful Gorgon's head and the three plumes which o'ershadow his helmet.

DICAEOPOLIS. No, no, he will get nothing, even though he gave me his buckler. Let

---

[106] The second day of the Dionysia or feasts of Bacchus, kept in the month Anthesterion (February), and called the Anthesteria. They lasted three days; the second being the Feast of Cups, the third the Feast of Pans. Vases, filled with grain of all kinds, were borne in procession and dedicated to Hermes.

him eat salt fish, while he shakes his plumes, and, if he comes here making any din, I shall call the inspectors. As for myself, I shall take away all these goods; I go home on thrushes' wings and black-birds' pinions.[107]

CHORUS. You see, citizens, you see the good fortune which this man owes to his prudence, to his profound wisdom. You see how, since he has concluded peace, he buys what is useful in the household and good to eat hot. All good things flow towards him unsought. Never will I welcome the god of war in my house; never shall he chant the "Harmodius" at my table;[108] he is a sot, who comes feasting with those who are overflowing with good things and brings all manner of mischief at his heels. He overthrows, ruins, rips open; 'tis vain to make him a thousand offers, "be seated, pray, drink this cup, proffered in all friendship," he burns our vine-stocks and brutally pours out the wine from our vineyards on the ground. This man, on the other hand, covers his table with a thousand dishes; proud of his good fortunes, he has had these feathers cast before his door to show us how he lives.

DICAEOPOLIS. Oh, Peace! companion of fair Aphrodite and of the sweet Graces, how charming are thy features and yet I never knew it! Would that Eros might join me to thee, Eros, crowned with roses as Zeuxis[109] shows him to us! Perhaps I seem somewhat old to you, but I am yet able to make you a threefold offering; despite my age I could plant a long row of vines for you; then beside these some tender cuttings from the fig; finally a young vine-stock, loaded with fruit and all around the field olive trees, which would furnish us with oil, wherewith to anoint us both at the New Moons.

HERALD. List, ye people! As was the custom of your forebears, empty a full pitcher of wine at the call of the trumpet; he, who first sees the bottom, shall get a wine-skin as round and plump as Ctesiphon's belly.

DICAEOPOLIS. Women, children, have you not heard? Faith! do you not heed the herald? Quick! let the hares boil and roast merrily; keep them a-turning; withdraw them from the flame; prepare the chaplets; reach me the skewers that I may spit the thrushes.

CHORUS. I envy you your wisdom and even more your good cheer.

DICAEOPOLIS. What then will you say when you see the thrushes roasting?

CHORUS. Ah! true indeed!

DICAEOPOLIS. Slave! stir up the fire.

CHORUS. See, how he knows his business, what a perfect cook! How well he understands the way to prepare a good dinner!

A HUSBANDMAN. Ah! woe is me!

DICAEOPOLIS. Heracles! What have we here?

HUSBANDMAN. A most miserable man.

DICAEOPOLIS. Keep your misery for yourself.

HUSBANDMAN. Ah! friend! since you alone are enjoying peace, grant me a part of your truce, were it but five years.

DICAEOPOLIS. What has happened to you?

HUSBANDMAN. I am ruined; I have lost a pair of steers.

DICAEOPOLIS. How?

---

[107] A parody on some verses from a lost poet.
[108] A feasting song in honour of Harmodius, the assassin of Hipparchus the Tyrant, son of Pisistratus.
[109] The celebrated painter, born in Heraclea, a contemporary of Aristophanes.

HUSBANDMAN. The Boeotians seized them at Phyle.[110]

DICAEOPOLIS. Ah! poor wretch! and yet you have not left off white?

HUSBANDMAN. Their dung made my wealth.

DICAEOPOLIS. What can I do in the matter?

HUSBANDMAN. Crying for my beasts has lost me my eyesight. Ah! if you care for poor Dercetes of Phyle, anoint mine eyes quickly with your balm of peace.

DICAEOPOLIS. But, my poor fellow, I do not practise medicine.

HUSBANDMAN. Come, I adjure you; perhaps I shall recover my steers.

DICAEOPOLIS. 'Tis impossible; away, go and whine to the disciples of Pittalus.[111]

HUSBANDMAN. Grant me but one drop of peace; pour it into this reedlet.

DICAEOPOLIS. No, not a particle; go a-weeping elsewhere.

HUSBANDMAN. Oh! oh! oh! my poor beasts!

CHORUS. This man has discovered the sweetest enjoyment in peace; he will share it with none.

DICAEOPOLIS. Pour honey over this tripe; set it before the fire to dry.

CHORUS. What lofty tones he uses! Did you hear him?

DICAEOPOLIS. Get the eels on the gridiron!

CHORUS. You are killing me with hunger; your smoke is choking your neighbours, and you split our ears with your bawling.

DICAEOPOLIS. Have this fried and let it be nicely browned.

A BRIDESMAID. Dicaeopolis! Dicaeopolis!

DICAEOPOLIS. Who are you?

BRIDESMAID. A young bridegroom sends you these viands from the marriage feast.

DICAEOPOLIS. Whoever he be, I thank him.

BRIDESMAID. And in return, he prays you to pour a glass of peace into this vase, that he may not have to go to the front and may stay at home to do his duty to his young wife.

DICAEOPOLIS. Take back, take back your viands; for a thousand drachmae I would not give a drop of peace; but who are you, pray?

BRIDESMAID. I am the bridesmaid; she wants to say something to you from the bride privately.

DICAEOPOLIS. Come, what do you wish to say? [THE BRIDESMAID *whispers in his ear.*] Ah! what a ridiculous demand! The bride burns with longing to keep by her her husband's weapon. Come! \bring hither my truce; to her alone will I give some of it, for she is a woman, and, as such, should not suffer under the war. Here, friend, reach hither your vial. And as to the manner of applying this balm, tell the bride, when a levy of soldiers is made to rub some in bed on her husband, where most needed. There, slave, take away my truce! Now, quick, bring me the wine-flagon, that I may fill up the drinking bowls!

CHORUS. I see a man, striding along apace, with knitted brows; he seems to us the bearer of terrible tidings.

HERALD. Oh! toils and battles, 'tis Lamachus!

LAMACHUS. What noise resounds around my dwelling, where shines the glint of arms.

HERALD. The Generals order you forthwith to take your battalions and your plumes, and, despite the snow, to go and guard our borders. They have learnt that a band of

---

[110] A deme and frontier fortress of Attica, near the Boeotian border.

[111] An Athenian physician of the day.

Boeotians intend taking advantage of the Feast of Cups to invade our country.

LAMACHUS. Ah! the Generals! they are numerous, but not good for much! It's cruel, not to be able to enjoy the feast!

DICAEOPOLIS. Oh! warlike host of Lamachus!

LAMACHUS. Wretch! do you dare to jeer me?

DICAEOPOLIS. Do you want to fight this four-winged Geryon?

LAMACHUS. Oh! oh! what fearful tidings!

DICAEOPOLIS. Ah! ah! I see another herald running up; what news does he bring me?

HERALD. Dicaeopolis!

DICAEOPOLIS. What is the matter?

HERALD. Come quickly to the feast and bring your basket and your cup; 'tis the priest of Bacchus who invites you. But hasten, the guests have been waiting for you a long while. All is ready—couches, tables, cushions, chaplets, perfumes, dainties and courtesans to boot; biscuits, cakes, sesame-bread, tarts, lovely dancing women, the sweetest charm of the festivity. But come with all haste.

LAMACHUS. Oh! hostile gods!

DICAEOPOLIS. This is not astounding; you have chosen this huge, great ugly Gorgon's head for your patron. You, shut the door, and let someone get ready the meal.

LAMACHUS. Slave! slave! my knapsack!

DICAEOPOLIS. Slave! slave! a basket!

LAMACHUS. Take salt and thyme, slave, and don't forget the onions.

DICAEOPOLIS. Get some fish for me; I cannot bear onions.

LAMACHUS. Slave, wrap me up a little stale salt meat in a fig-leaf.

DICAEOPOLIS. And for me some good greasy tripe in a fig-leaf; I will have it cooked here.

LAMACHUS. Bring me the plumes for my helmet.

DICAEOPOLIS. Bring me wild pigeons and thrushes.

LAMACHUS. How white and beautiful are these ostrich feathers!

DICAEOPOLIS. How fat and well browned is the flesh of this wood-pigeon!

LAMACHUS. Bring me the case for my triple plume.

DICAEOPOLIS. Pass me over that dish of hare.

LAMACHUS. OH! the moths have eaten the hair of my crest.

DICAEOPOLIS. I shall always eat hare before dinner.

LAMACHUS. Hi! friend! try not to scoff at my armor?

DICAEOPOLIS. Hi! friend! will you kindly not stare at my thrushes.

LAMACHUS. Hi! friend! will you kindly not address me.

DICAEOPOLIS. I do not address you; I am scolding my slave. Shall we wager and submit the matter to Lamachus, which of the two is the best to eat, a locust or a thrush?

LAMACHUS. Insolent hound!

DICAEOPOLIS. He much prefers the locusts.

LAMACHUS. Slave, unhook my spear and bring it to me.

DICAEOPOLIS. Slave, slave, take the sausage from the fire and bring it to me.

LAMACHUS. Come, let me draw my spear from its sheath. Hold it, slave, hold it tight.

DICAEOPOLIS. And you, slave, grip, grip well hold of the skewer.

LAMACHUS. Slave, the bracings for my shield.

DICAEOPOLIS. Pull the loaves out of the oven and bring me these bracings of my stomach.

LAMACHUS. My round buckler with the Gorgon's head.

DICAEOPOLIS. My round cheese-cake.

LAMACHUS. What clumsy wit!

DICAEOPOLIS. What delicious cheese-cake!

LAMACHUS. Pour oil on the buckler. Hah! hah! I can see reflected there an old man who will be accused of cowardice.

DICAEOPOLIS. Pour honey on the cake. Hah! hah! I can see an old man who makes Lamachus of the Gorgon's head weep with rage.

LAMACHUS. Slave, full war armour.

DICAEOPOLIS. Slave, my beaker; that is *my* armour.

LAMACHUS. With this I hold my ground with any foe.

DICAEOPOLIS. And I with this with any tosspot.

LAMACHUS. Fasten the strappings to the buckler; personally I shall carry the knapsack.

DICAEOPOLIS. Pack the dinner well into the basket; personally I shall carry the cloak.

LAMACHUS. Slave, take up the buckler and let's be off. It is snowing! Ah! 'tis a question of facing the winter.

DICAEOPOLIS. Take up the basket, 'tis a question of getting to the feast.

CHORUS. We wish you both joy on your journeys, which differ so much. One goes to mount guard and freeze, while the other will drink, crowned with flowers, and then sleep with a young beauty, who will excite him readily.

I say it freely; may Zeus confound Antimachus, the poet-historian, the son of Psacas! When Choregus at the Lenaea, alas! alas! he dismissed me dinnerless. May I see him devouring with his eyes a cuttle-fish, just served, well cooked, hot and properly salted; and the moment that he stretches his hand to help himself, may a dog seize it and run off with it. Such is my first wish. I also hope for him a misfortune at night. That returning all-fevered from horse practice, he may meet an Orestes,[112] mad with drink, who breaks open his head; that wishing to seize a stone, he, in the dark, may pick up a fresh stool, hurl his missile, miss aim and hit Cratinus.[113]

SLAVE OF LAMACHUS. Slaves of Lamachus! Water, water in a little pot! Make it warm, get ready cloths, cerate greasy wool and bandages for his ankle. In leaping a ditch, the master has hurt himself against a stake; he has dislocated and twisted his ankle, broken his head by falling on a stone, while his Gorgon shot far away from his buckler. His mighty braggadocio plume rolled on the ground; at this sight he uttered these doleful words, "Radiant star, I gaze on thee for the last time; my eyes close to all light, I die." Having said this, he falls into the water, gets out again, meets some runaways and pursues the robbers with his spear at their backsides.[114] But here he comes, himself. Get the door open.

LAMACHUS. Oh! heavens! oh! heavens! What cruel pain! I faint, I tremble! Alas! I die! the foe's lance has struck me! But what would hurt me most would be for Dicaeopolis to see me wounded thus and laugh at my ill-fortune.

DICAEOPOLIS. [*enters with two courtesans.*] Oh! my gods! what bosoms! Hard as a quince! Come, my treasures, give me voluptuous kisses! Glue your lips to mine. Haha! I was the first to empty my cup.

---

[112] An allusion to the paroxysms of rage, as represented in many tragedies familiar to an Athenian audience, of Orestes, the son of Agamemnon, after he had killed his mother.

[113] No doubt the comic poet, rival of Aristophanes.

[114] Unexpected wind-up of the story. Aristophanes intends to deride the boasting of Lamachus, who was always ascribing to himself most unlikely exploits.

LAMACHUS. Oh! cruel fate! how I suffer! accursed wounds!

DICAEOPOLIS. Hah! hah! hail! Knight Lamachus! [*embraces* LAMACHUS.]

LAMACHUS. By the hostile gods! [*bites* DICAEOPOLIS.]

DICAEOPOLIS. Ah! Great gods!

LAMACHUS. Why do you embrace me?

DICAEOPOLIS. And why do you bite me?

LAMACHUS. 'Twas a cruel score I was paying back!

DICAEOPOLIS. Scores are not evened at the Feast of Cups!

LAMACHUS. Oh! Paean, Paean!

DICAEOPOLIS. But to-day is not the feast of Paean.

LAMACHUS. Oh! support my leg, do; ah! hold it tenderly, my friends!

DICAEOPOLIS. And you, my darlings, take hold of this, both of you!

LAMACHUS. This blow with the stone makes me dizzy; my sight grows dim.

DICAEOPOLIS. For myself, I want to get to bed; I am bursting with lustfulness, I want to be bundling in the dark.

LAMACHUS. Carry me to the surgeon Pittalus.

DICAEOPOLIS. Take me to the judges. Where is the king of the feast? The wine-skin is mine!

LAMACHUS. That spear has pierced my bones; what torture I endure!

DICAEOPOLIS. You see this empty cup! I triumph! I triumph!

CHORUS. Old man, I come at your bidding! You triumph! you triumph!

DICAEOPOLIS. Again I have brimmed my cup with unmixed wine and drained it at a draught!

CHORUS. You triumph then, brave champion; thine is the wine-skin!

DICAEOPOLIS. Follow me, singing "Triumph! Triumph!"

CHORUS. Aye! we will sing of thee, thee and thy sacred wine-skin, and we all, as we follow thee, will repeat in thine honour, "Triumph, Triumph!"

# THE CLOUDS

## INTRODUCTION

The satire in this, one of the best known of all Aristophanes' comedies, is directed against the new schools of philosophy, or perhaps we should rather say dialectic, which had lately been introduced, mostly from abroad, at Athens. The doctrines held up to ridicule are those of the 'Sophists'—such men as Thrasymachus from Chalcedon in Bithynia, Gorgias from Leontini in Sicily, Protagoras from Abdera in Thrace, and other foreign scholars and rhetoricians who had flocked to Athens as the intellectual centre of the Hellenic world. Strange to say, Socrates of all people, the avowed enemy and merciless critic of these men and their methods, is taken as their representative, and personally attacked with pitiless raillery. Presumably this was merely because he was the most prominent and noteworthy teacher and thinker of the day, while his grotesque personal appearance and startling eccentricities of behaviour gave a ready handle to caricature. Neither the author nor his audience took the trouble, or were likely to take the trouble, to discriminate nicely; there was, of course, a general resemblance between the Socratic 'elenchos' and the methods of the new practitioners of dialectic; and this was enough for stage purposes. However unjustly, Socrates is taken as typical of the newfangled sophistical teachers, just as in 'The Acharnians' Lamachus, with his Gorgon shield, is introduced as representative of the War party, though that general was not specially responsible for the continuance of hostilities more than anybody else.

Aristophanes' point of view, as a member of the aristocratical party and a fine old Conservative, is that these Sophists, as the professors of the new education had come to be called, and Socrates as their protagonist, were insincere and dangerous innovators, corrupting morals, persuading young men to despise the old-fashioned, home-grown virtues of the State and teaching a system of false and pernicious tricks of verbal fence whereby anything whatever could be proved, and the worse be made to seem the better— provided always sufficient payment were forthcoming. True, Socrates refused to take money from his pupils, and made it his chief reproach against the lecturing Sophists that they received fees; but what of that? The Comedian cannot pay heed to such fine distinctions, but belabours the whole tribe with indiscriminate raillery and scurrility.

The play was produced at the Great Dionysia in 423 B.C., but proved unsuccessful, Cratinus and Amipsias being awarded first and second prize. This is said to have been due to the intrigues and influence of Alcibiades, who resented the caricature of himself presented in the sporting Phidippides. A second edition of the drama was apparently produced some years later, to which the 'Parabasis' of the play as we possess it must belong, as it refers to events subsequent to the date named.

The plot is briefly as follows: Strepsiades, a wealthy country gentleman, has been brought to penury and deeply involved in debt by the extravagance and horsy tastes of his son Phidippides. Having heard of the wonderful new art of argument, the royal road to success in litigation, discovered by the Sophists, he hopes that, if only he can enter the 'Phrontisterion,' or Thinking-Shop, of Socrates, he will learn how to turn the tables on his creditors and avoid paying the debts which are dragging him down. He joins the school accordingly, but is found too old and stupid to profit by the lessons. So his son Phidippides is substituted as a more promising pupil. The latter takes to the new learning like a duck to water, and soon shows what progress he has made by beating his father and demonstrating that he is justified by all laws, divine and human, in what he is doing. This opens the old man's eyes, who sets fire to the 'Phrontisterion,' and the play ends in a great conflagration of this home of humbug.

## DRAMATIS PERSONAE

STREPSIADES
PHIDIPPIDES
SERVANT OF STREPSIADES
SOCRATES
DISCIPLES OF SOCRATES
JUST DISCOURSE
UNJUST DISCOURSE
PASIAS, *a Money-lender*
PASIAS' WITNESS
AMYNIAS, *another Money-lender*
CHAEREPHON
CHORUS OF CLOUDS

SCENE: *A sleeping-room in Strepsiades' house; then in front of Socrates' house.*

# THE CLOUDS

STREPSIADES.[115] Great gods! will these nights never end? will daylight never come? I heard the cock crow long ago and my slaves are snoring still! Ah! 'twas not so formerly. Curses on the War! has it not done me ills enough? Now I may not even chastise my own slaves.[116] Again there's this brave lad, who never wakes the whole long night, but, wrapped in his five coverlets, farts away to his heart's content. Come! let me nestle in well and snore too, if it be possible ... oh! misery, 'tis vain to think of sleep with all these expenses, this stable, these debts, which are devouring me, thanks to this fine cavalier, who only knows how to look after his long locks, to show himself off in his chariot and to dream of horses! And I, I am nearly dead, when I see the moon bringing the third decade in her train[117] and my liability falling due.... Slave! light the lamp and bring me my tablets. Who are all my creditors? Let me see and reckon up the interest. What is it I owe? ... Twelve minae to Pasias.... What! twelve minae to Pasias? ... Why did I borrow these? Ah! I know! 'Twas to buy that thoroughbred, which cost me so dear.[118] How I should have prized the stone that had blinded him!

PHIDIPPIDES. [*in his sleep.*] That's not fair, Philo! Drive your chariot straight,[119] I say.

STREPSIADES. 'Tis this that is destroying me. He raves about horses, even in his sleep.

PHIDIPPIDES. [*still sleeping.*] How many times round the track is the race for the chariots of war?[120]

STREPSIADES. 'Tis your own father you are driving to death ... to ruin. Come! what debt comes next, after that of Pasias? ... Three minae to Amynias for a chariot and its two wheels.

PHIDIPPIDES. [*still asleep.*] Give the horse a good roll in the dust and lead him home.

STREPSIADES. Ah! wretched boy! 'tis my money that you are making roll. My creditors have distrained on my goods, and here are others again, who demand security for their interest.

PHIDIPPIDES. [*awaking.*] What is the matter with you, father, that you groan and turn about the whole night through?

STREPSIADES. I have a bum-bailiff in the bedclothes biting me.

PHIDIPPIDES. For pity's sake, let me have a little sleep.

STREPSIADES. Very well, sleep on! but remember that all these debts will fall back on your shoulders. Oh! curses on the go-between who made me marry your mother! I lived so happily in the country, a commonplace, everyday life, but a good

---

[115] He is in one bed and his son is in another; slaves are sleeping near them. It is night-time.

[116] The punishment most frequently inflicted upon slaves in the towns was to send them into the country to work in the fields, but at the period when the 'Clouds' was presented, 424 B.C., the invasions of the Peloponnesians forbade the pursuit of agriculture. Moreover, there existed the fear, that if the slaves were punished too harshly, they might go over to the enemy.

[117] Among the Greeks, each month was divided into three decades. The last of the month was called [Greek: *ene kai nea*], the day of the old and the new or the day of the new moon, and on that day interest, which it was customary to pay monthly, became due.

[118] Literally, the horse marked with the [Greek: *koppa*] ([Symbol: Letter '*koppa*']), a letter of the older Greek alphabet, afterwards disused, which distinguished the thoroughbreds.

[119] Phidippides dreams that he is driving in a chariot race, and that an opponent is trying to cut into his track.

[120] There was a prize specially reserved for war-chariots in the games of the Athenian hippodrome; being heavier than the chariots generally used, they doubtless had to cover a lesser number of laps, which explains Phidippides' question.

and easy one—had not a trouble, not a care, was rich in bees, in sheep and in olives. Then forsooth I must marry the niece of Megacles, the son of Megacles; I belonged to the country, she was from the town; she was a haughty, extravagant woman, a true Coesyra.[121] On the nuptial day, when I lay beside her, I was reeking of the dregs of the wine-cup, of cheese and of wool; she was redolent with essences, saffron, tender kisses, the love of spending, of good cheer and of wanton delights. I will not say she did nothing; no, she worked hard ... to ruin me, and pretending all the while merely to be showing her the cloak she had woven for me, I said, "Wife, you go too fast about your work, your threads are too closely woven and you use far too much wool."

A SLAVE. There is no more oil in the lamp.

STREPSIADES. Why then did you light such a guzzling lamp? Come here, I am going to beat you!

SLAVE. What for?

STREPSIADES. Because you have put in too thick a wick.... Later, when we had this boy, what was to be his name? 'Twas the cause of much quarrelling with my loving wife. She insisted on having some reference to a horse in his name, that he should be called Xanthippus, Charippus or Callippides.[122] I wanted to name him Phidonides after his grandfather.[123] We disputed long, and finally agreed to style him Phidippides....[124] She used to fondle and coax him, saying, "Oh! what a joy it will be to me when you have grown up, to see you, like my father, Megacles,[125] clothed in purple and standing up straight in your chariot driving your steeds toward the town." And I would say to him, "When, like your father, you will go, dressed in a skin, to fetch back your goats from Phelleus."[126] Alas! he never listened to me and his madness for horses has shattered my fortune. But by dint of thinking the livelong night, I have discovered a road to salvation, both miraculous and divine. If he will but follow it, I shall be out of my trouble! First, however, he must be awakened, but let it be done as gently as possible. How shall I manage it? Phidippides! my little Phidippides!

PHIDIPPIDES. What is it, father!

STREPSIADES. Kiss me and give me your hand.

PHIDIPPIDES. There! What's it all about?

STREPSIADES. Tell me! do you love me?

PHIDIPPIDES. By Posidon, the equestrian Posidon! yes, I swear I do.

STREPSIADES. Oh, do not, I pray you, invoke this god of horses; 'tis he who is the cause of all my cares. But if you really love me, and with your whole heart, my boy, believe me.

PHIDIPPIDES. Believe you? about what?

STREPSIADES. Alter your habits forthwith and go and learn what I tell you.

PHIDIPPIDES. Say on, what are your orders?

---

[121] The wife of Alcmaeon, a descendant of Nestor, who, driven from Messenia by the Heraclidae, came to settle in Athens in the twelfth century, and was the ancestor of the great family of the Alcmaeonidae, Pericles and Alcibiades belonged to it.

[122] The Greek word for horse is [Greek: hippos.]

[123] Derived from [Greek: pheidesthai], to save.

[124] The name Phidippides contains both words, [Greek: hippos], horse, and [Greek: pheidesthai], to save, and was therefore a compromise arrived at between the two parents.

[125] The heads of the family of the Alcmaeonidae bore the name of Megacles from generation to generation.

[126] A mountain in Attica.

STREPSIADES. Will you obey me ever so little?

PHIDIPPIDES. By Bacchus, I will obey you.

STREPSIADES. Very well then! Look this way. Do you see that little door and that little house?[127]

PHIDIPPIDES. Yes, father. But what are you driving at?

STREPSIADES. That is the school of wisdom. There, they prove that we are coals enclosed on all sides under a vast extinguisher, which is the sky.[128] If well paid,[129] these men also teach one how to gain law-suits, whether they be just or not.

PHIDIPPIDES. What do they call themselves?

STREPSIADES. I do not know exactly, but they are deep thinkers and most admirable people.

PHIDIPPIDES. Bah! the wretches! I know them; you mean those quacks with livid faces,[130] those barefoot fellows, such as that miserable Socrates and Chaerephon.[131]

STREPSIADES. Silence! say nothing foolish! If you desire your father not to die of hunger, join their company and let your horses go.

PHIDIPPIDES. No, by Bacchus! even though you gave me the pheasants that Leogoras rears.

STREPSIADES. Oh! my beloved son, I beseech you, go and follow their teachings.

PHIDIPPIDES. And what is it I should learn?

STREPSIADES. 'Twould seem they have two courses of reasoning, the true and the false, and that, thanks to the false, the worst law-suits can be gained. If then you learn this science, which is false, I shall not pay an obolus of all the debts I have contracted on your account.

PHIDIPPIDES. No, I will not do it. I should no longer dare to look at our gallant horsemen, when I had so tarnished my fair hue of honour.

STREPSIADES. Well then, by Demeter! I will no longer support you, neither you, nor your team, nor your saddle-horse. Go and hang yourself, I turn you out of house and home.

PHIDIPPIDES. My uncle Megacles will not leave me without horses; I shall go to him and laugh at your anger.

STREPSIADES. One rebuff shall not dishearten me. With the help of the gods I will enter this school and learn myself. But at my age, memory has gone and the mind is slow to grasp things. How can all these fine distinctions, these subtleties be learned? Bah! why should I dally thus instead of rapping at the door? Slave, slave! [*He knocks and calls.*]

A DISCIPLE. A plague on you! Who are you?

STREPSIADES. Strepsiades, the son of Phido, of the deme of Cicynna.

DISCIPLE. 'Tis for sure only an ignorant and illiterate fellow who lets drive at the door with such kicks. You have brought on a miscarriage—of an idea!

STREPSIADES. Pardon me, pray; for I live far away from here in the country. But tell me, what was the idea that miscarried?

DISCIPLE. I may not tell it to any but a disciple.

---

[127] Aristophanes represents everything belonging to Socrates as being mean, even down to his dwelling.

[128] Crates ascribes the same doctrine in one of his plays to the Pythagorean Hippo, of Samos.

[129] This is pure calumny. Socrates accepted no payment.

[130] Here the poet confounds Socrates' disciples with the Stoics. Contrary to the text, Socrates held that a man should care for his bodily health.

[131] One of Socrates' pupils.

STREPSIADES. Then tell me without fear, for I have come to study among you.

DISCIPLE. Very well then, but reflect, that these are mysteries. Lately, a flea bit Chaerephon on the brow and then from there sprang on to the head of Socrates. Socrates asked Chaerephon, "How many times the length of its legs does a flea jump?"

STREPSIADES. And how ever did he set about measuring it?

DISCIPLE. Oh! 'twas most ingenious! He melted some wax, seized the flea and dipped its two feet in the wax, which, when cooled, left them shod with true Persian buskins.[132] These he slipped off and with them measured the distance.

STREPSIADES. Ah! great Zeus! what a brain! what subtlety!

DISCIPLE. I wonder what then would you say, if you knew another of Socrates' contrivances?

STREPSIADES. What is it? Pray tell me.

DISCIPLE. Chaerephon of the deme of Sphettia asked him whether he thought a gnat buzzed through its proboscis or through its rear.

STREPSIADES. And what did he say about the gnat?

DISCIPLE. He said that the gut of the gnat was narrow, and that, in passing through this tiny passage, the air is driven with force towards the breech; then after this slender channel, it encountered the rump, which was distended like a trumpet, and there it resounded sonorously.

STREPSIADES. So the rear of a gnat is a trumpet. Oh! what a splendid discovery! Thrice happy Socrates! 'Twould not be difficult to succeed in a law-suit, knowing so much about the gut of a gnat!

DISCIPLE. Not long ago a lizard caused him the loss of a sublime thought.

STREPSIADES. In what way, an it please you?

DISCIPLE. One night, when he was studying the course of the moon and its revolutions and was gazing open-mouthed at the heavens, a lizard shitted upon him from the top of the roof.

STREPSIADES. This lizard, that relieved itself over Socrates, tickles me.

DISCIPLE. Yesternight we had nothing to eat.

STREPSIADES. Well! What did he contrive, to secure you some supper?

DISCIPLE. He spread over the table a light layer of cinders, bending an iron rod the while; then he took up a pair of compasses and at the same moment unhooked a piece of the victim which was hanging in the palaestra.[133]

STREPSIADES. And we still dare to admire Thales![134] Open, open this home of knowledge to me quickly! Haste, haste to show me Socrates; I long to become his disciple. But do, do open the door. [*The disciple admits* STREPSIADES.] Ah! by Heracles! what country are those animals from?

DISCIPLE. Why, what are you astonished at? What do you think they resemble?

---

[132] Female footwear. They were a sort of light slipper and white in colour.

[133] He calls off their attention by pretending to show them a geometrical problem and seizes the opportunity to steal something for supper. The young men who gathered together in the palaestra, or gymnastic school, were wont there to offer sacrifices to the gods before beginning the exercises. The offerings consisted of smaller victims, such as lambs, fowl, geese, etc., and the flesh afterwards was used for their meal (*vide* Plato in the 'Lysias'). It is known that Socrates taught wherever he might happen to be, in the palaestra as well as elsewhere.

[134] The first of the seven sages, born at Miletus.

STREPSIADES. The captives of Pylos.[135] But why do they look so fixedly on the ground?

DISCIPLE. They are seeking for what is below the ground.

STREPSIADES. Ah! 'tis onions they are seeking. Do not give yourselves so much trouble; I know where there are some, fine and large ones. But what are those fellows doing, who are bent all double?

DISCIPLE. They are sounding the abysses of Tartarus.[136]

STREPSIADES. And what is their rump looking at in the heavens?

DISCIPLE. It is studying astronomy on its own account. But come in; so that the master may not find us here.

STREPSIADES. Not yet, not yet; let them not change their position. I want to tell them my own little matter.

DISCIPLE. But they may not stay too long in the open air and away from school.

STREPSIADES. In the name of all the gods, what is that? Tell me. [*Pointing to a celestial globe.*]

DISCIPLE. That is astronomy.

STREPSIADES. And that? [*Pointing to a map.*]

DISCIPLE. Geometry.

STREPSIADES. What is that used for?

DISCIPLE. To measure the land.

STREPSIADES. But that is apportioned by lot.[137]

DISCIPLE. No, no, I mean the entire earth.

STREPSIADES. Ah! what a funny thing! How generally useful indeed is this invention!

DISCIPLE. There is the whole surface of the earth. Look! Here is Athens.

STREPSIADES. Athens! you are mistaken; I see no courts sitting.[138]

DISCIPLE. Nevertheless it is really and truly the Attic territory.

STREPSIADES. And where are my neighbours of Cicynna?

DISCIPLE. They live here. This is Euboea; you see this island, that is so long and narrow.

STREPSIADES. I know. 'Tis we and Pericles, who have stretched it by dint of squeezing it.[139] And where is Lacedaemon?

DISCIPLE. Lacedaemon? Why, here it is, look.

STREPSIADES. How near it is to us! Think it well over, it must be removed to a greater distance.

DISCIPLE. But, by Zeus, that is not possible.

STREPSIADES. Then, woe to you! And who is this man suspended up in a basket?

DISCIPLE. 'Tis *he himself.*

STREPSIADES. Who himself?

DISCIPLE. Socrates.

STREPSIADES. Socrates! Oh! I pray you, call him right loudly for me.

DISCIPLE. Call him yourself; I have no time to waste.

---

[135] Because of their wretched appearance. The Laconians, blockaded in Sphacteria, had suffered sorely from famine.

[136] In fact, this was one of the chief accusations brought against Socrates by Miletus and Anytus; he was reproached for probing into the mysteries of nature.

[137] When the Athenians captured a town, they divided its lands by lot among the poorer Athenian citizens.

[138] An allusion to the Athenian love of law-suits and litigation.

[139] When originally conquered by Pericles, the island of Euboea, off the coasts of Boeotia and Attica, had been treated with extreme harshness.

STREPSIADES. Socrates! my little Socrates!

SOCRATES. Mortal, what do you want with me?

STREPSIADES. First, what are you doing up there? Tell me, I beseech you.

SOCRATES. I traverse the air and contemplate the sun.

STREPSIADES. Thus 'tis not on the solid ground, but from the height of this basket, that you slight the gods, if indeed....[140]

SOCRATES. I have to suspend my brain and mingle the subtle essence of my mind with this air, which is of the like nature, in order to clearly penetrate the things of heaven.[141] I should have discovered nothing, had I remained on the ground to consider from below the things that are above; for the earth by its force attracts the sap of the mind to itself. 'Tis just the same with the water-cress.[142]

STREPSIADES. What? Does the mind attract the sap of the water-cress? Ah! my dear little Socrates, come down to me! I have come to ask you for lessons.

SOCRATES. And for what lessons?

STREPSIADES. I want to learn how to speak. I have borrowed money, and my merciless creditors do not leave me a moment's peace; all my goods are at stake.

SOCRATES. And how was it you did not see that you were getting so much into debt?

STREPSIADES. My ruin has been the madness for horses, a most rapacious evil; but teach me one of your two methods of reasoning, the one whose object is not to repay anything, and, may the gods bear witness, that I am ready to pay any fee you may name.

SOCRATES. By which gods will you swear? To begin with, the gods are not a coin current with us.

STREPSIADES. But what do you swear by then? By the iron money of Byzantium?[143]

SOCRATES. Do you really wish to know the truth of celestial matters?

STREPSIADES. Why, truly, if 'tis possible.

SOCRATES. ... and to converse with the clouds, who are our genii?

STREPSIADES. Without a doubt.

SOCRATES. Then be seated on this sacred couch.

STREPSIADES. I am seated.

SOCRATES. Now take this chaplet.

STREPSIADES. Why a chaplet? Alas! Socrates, would you sacrifice me, like Athamas?[144]

SOCRATES. No, these are the rites of initiation.

STREPSIADES. And what is it I am to gain?

SOCRATES. You will become a thorough rattle-pate, a hardened old stager, the fine flour of the talkers.... But come, keep quiet.

STREPSIADES. By Zeus! You lie not! Soon I shall be nothing but wheat-flour, if you powder me in this fashion.[145]

SOCRATES. Silence, old man, give heed to the prayers.... Oh! most mighty king, the

---

[0] Is about to add, "you believe in them at all," but checks himself.

[1] This was the doctrine of Anaximenes.

[2] The scholiast explains that water-cress robs all plants that grow in its vicinity of their moisture and that they consequently soon wither and die.

[3] In the other Greek towns, the smaller coins were of copper.

[4] Athamas, King of Thebes. An allusion to a tragedy by Sophocles, in which Athamas is dragged before the altar of Zeus with his head circled with a chaplet, to be there sacrificed; he is, however, saved by Heracles.

[5] No doubt Socrates sprinkled flour over the head of Strepsiades in the same manner as was done with the sacrificial victims.

boundless air, that keepest the earth suspended in space, thou bright Aether and ye venerable goddesses, the Clouds, who carry in your loins the thunder and the lightning, arise, ye sovereign powers and manifest yourselves in the celestial spheres to the eyes of the sage.

STREPSIADES. Not yet! Wait a bit, till I fold my mantle double, so as not to get wet. And to think that I did not even bring my travelling cap! What a misfortune!

SOCRATES. Come, oh! Clouds, whom I adore, come and show yourselves to this man, whether you be resting on the sacred summits of Olympus, crowned with hoar-frost, or tarrying in the gardens of Ocean, your father, forming sacred choruses with the Nymphs; whether you be gathering the waves of the Nile in golden vases or dwelling in the Maeotic marsh or on the snowy rocks of Mimas, hearken to my prayer and accept my offering. May these sacrifices be pleasing to you.

CHORUS. Eternal Clouds, let us appear, let us arise from the roaring depths of Ocean, our father; let us fly towards the lofty mountains, spread our damp wings over their forest-laden summits, whence we will dominate the distant valleys, the harvest fed by the sacred earth, the murmur of the divine streams and the resounding waves of the sea, which the unwearying orb lights up with its glittering beams. But let us shake off the rainy fogs, which hide our immortal beauty and sweep the earth from afar with our gaze.

SOCRATES. Oh, venerated goddesses, yes, you are answering my call! [to STREPSIADES.] Did you hear their voices mingling with the awful growling of the thunder?

STREPSIADES. Oh! adorable Clouds, I revere you and I too am going to let off my thunder, so greatly has your own affrighted me. Faith! whether permitted or not, I must, I must shit!

SOCRATES. No scoffing; do not copy those accursed comic poets. Come, silence! a numerous host of goddesses approaches with songs.

CHORUS. Virgins, who pour forth the rains, let us move toward Attica, the rich country of Pallas, the home of the brave; let us visit the dear land of Cecrops, where the secret rites[146] are celebrated, where the mysterious sanctuary flies open to the initiate.... What victims are offered there to the deities of heaven! What glorious temples! What statues! What holy prayers to the rulers of Olympus! At every season nothing but sacred festivals, garlanded victims, are to be seen. Then Spring brings round again the joyous feasts of Dionysus, the harmonious contests of the choruses and the serious melodies of the flute.

STREPSIADES. By Zeus! Tell me, Socrates, I pray you, who are these women, whose language is so solemn; can they be demigoddesses?

SOCRATES. Not at all. They are the Clouds of heaven, great goddesses for the lazy; to them we owe all, thoughts, speeches, trickery, roguery, boasting, lies, sagacity.

STREPSIADES. Ah! that was why, as I listened to them, my mind spread out its wings; it burns to babble about trifles, to maintain worthless arguments, to voice its petty reasons, to contradict, to tease some opponent. But are they not going to show themselves? I should like to see them, were it possible.

SOCRATES. Well, look this way in the direction of Parnes;[147] I already see those who are slowly descending.

---

[146] The mysteries of Eleusis celebrated in the Temple of Demeter.
[147] A mountain of Attica, north of Athens.

STREPSIADES. But where, where? Show them to me.

SOCRATES. They are advancing in a throng, following an oblique path across the dales and thickets.

STREPSIADES. 'Tis strange! I can see nothing.

SOCRATES. There, close to the entrance.

STREPSIADES. Hardly, if at all, can I distinguish them.

SOCRATES. You *must* see them clearly now, unless your eyes are filled with gum as thick as pumpkins.

STREPSIADES. Aye, undoubtedly! Oh! the venerable goddesses! Why, they fill up the entire stage.

SOCRATES. And you did not know, you never suspected, that they were goddesses?

STREPSIADES. No, indeed; methought the Clouds were only fog, dew and vapour.

SOCRATES. But what you certainly do not know is that they are the support of a crowd of quacks, both the diviners, who were sent to Thurium,[148] the notorious physicians, the well-combed fops, who load their fingers with rings down to the nails, and the baggarts, who write dithyrambic verses, all these are idlers whom the Clouds provide a living for, because they sing them in their verses.

STREPSIADES. 'Tis then for this that they praise "the rapid flight of the moist clouds, which veil the brightness of day" and "the waving locks of the hundred-headed Typho" and "the impetuous tempests, which float through the heavens, like birds of prey with aerial wings, loaded with mists" and "the rains, the dew, which the clouds outpour."[149] As a reward for these fine phrases they bolt well-grown, tasty mullet and delicate thrushes.

SOCRATES. Yes, thanks to these. And is it not right and meet?

STREPSIADES. Tell me then why, if these really are the Clouds, they so very much resemble mortals. This is not their usual form.

SOCRATES. What are they like then?

STREPSIADES. I don't know exactly; well, they are like great packs of wool, but not like women—no, not in the least.... And these have noses.

SOCRATES. Answer my questions.

STREPSIADES. Willingly! Go on, I am listening.

SOCRATES. Have you not sometimes seen clouds in the sky like a centaur, a leopard, a wolf or a bull?

STREPSIADES. Why, certainly I have, but what then?

SOCRATES. They take what metamorphosis they like. If they see a debauchee with long flowing locks and hairy as a beast, like the son of Xenophantes,[150] they take the form of a Centaur[151] in derision of his shameful passion.

STREPSIADES. And when they see Simon, that thiever of public money, what do they do then?

SOCRATES. To picture him to the life, they turn at once into wolves.

STREPSIADES. So that was why yesterday, when they saw Cleonymus,[152] who cast

---

[148] Sybaris, a town of Magna Graecia (Lucania), destroyed by the Crotoniates in 709 B.C., was rebuilt by the Athenians under the name of Thurium in 444 B.C. Ten diviners had been sent with the Athenian settlers.

[149] A parody of the dithyrambic style.

[150] Hieronymus, a dithyrambic poet and reputed an infamous pederast.

[151] When guests at the nuptials of Pirithous, King of the Lapithae, and Hippodamia, they wanted to carry off and violate the bride. That, according to legend, was the origin of their war against the Lapithae. Hieronymus is likened to the Centaurs on account of his bestial passion.

[152] A general, incessantly scoffed at by Aristophanes because of his cowardice.

away his buckler because he is the veriest poltroon amongst men, they changed into deer.

SOCRATES. And to-day they have seen Clisthenes;[153] you see ... they are women.

STREPSIADES. Hail, sovereign goddesses, and if ever you have let your celestial voice be heard by mortal ears, speak to me, oh! speak to me, ye all-powerful queens.

CHORUS. Hail! veteran of the ancient times, you who burn to instruct yourself in fine language. And you, great high-priest of subtle nonsense, tell us your desire. To you and Prodicus[154] alone of all the hollow orationers of to-day have we lent an ear—to Prodicus, because of his knowledge and his great wisdom, and to you, because you walk with head erect, a confident look, barefooted, resigned to everything and proud of our protection.

STREPSIADES. Oh! Earth! What august utterances! how sacred! how wondrous!

SOCRATES. That is because these are the only goddesses; all the rest are pure myth.

STREPSIADES. But by the Earth! is our Father, Zeus, the Olympian, not a god?

SOCRATES. Zeus! what Zeus? Are you mad? There is no Zeus.

STREPSIADES. What are you saying now? Who causes the rain to fall? Answer me that!

SOCRATES. Why, 'tis these, and I will prove it. Have you ever seen it raining without clouds? Let Zeus then cause rain with a clear sky and without their presence!

STREPSIADES. By Apollo! that is powerfully argued! For my own part, I always thought it was Zeus pissing into a sieve. But tell me, who is it makes the thunder, which I so much dread?

SOCRATES. 'Tis these, when they roll one over the other.

STREPSIADES. But how can that be? you most daring among men!

SOCRATES. Being full of water, and forced to move along, they are of necessity precipitated in rain, being fully distended with moisture from the regions where they have been floating; hence they bump each other heavily and burst with great noise.

STREPSIADES. But is it not Zeus who forces them to move?

SOCRATES. Not at all; 'tis aerial Whirlwind.

STREPSIADES. The Whirlwind! ah! I did not know that. So Zeus, it seems, has no existence, and 'tis the Whirlwind that reigns in his stead? But you have not yet told me what makes the roll of the thunder?

SOCRATES. Have you not understood me then? I tell you, that the Clouds, when full of rain, bump against one another, and that, being inordinately swollen out, they burst with a great noise.

STREPSIADES. How can you make me credit that?

SOCRATES. Take yourself as an example. When you have heartily gorged on stew at the Panathenaea, you get throes of stomach-ache and then suddenly your belly resounds with prolonged growling.

STREPSIADES. Yes, yes, by Apollo! I suffer, I get colic, then the stew sets a-growling like thunder and finally bursts forth with a terrific noise. At first, 'tis but a little gurgling *pappax, pappax!* then it increases, *papapappax!* and when I seek relief, why, 'tis thunder indeed, *papapappax! pappax!! papapappax!!!* just like the clouds.

SOCRATES. Well then, reflect what a noise is produced by your belly, which is but

---

[153] Aristophanes frequently mentions him as an effeminate and debauched character.

[154] A celebrated sophist, born at Ceos, and a disciple of Protagoras. When sent on an embassy by his compatriots to Athens, he there publicly preached on eloquence, and had for his disciples Euripides, Isocrates and even Socrates. His "fifty drachmae lecture" has been much spoken of; that sum had to be paid to hear it.

small. Shall not the air, which is boundless, produce these mighty claps of thunder?

STREPSIADES. But tell me this. Whence comes the lightning, the dazzling flame, which at times consumes the man it strikes, at others hardly singes him. Is it not plain, that 'tis Zeus hurling it at the perjurers?

SOCRATES. Out upon the fool! the driveller! he still savours of the golden age! If Zeus strikes at the perjurers, why has he not blasted Simon, Cleonymus and Theorus?[155] Of a surety, greater perjurers cannot exist. No, he strikes his own Temple, and Sunium, the promontory of Athens,[156] and the towering oaks. Now, why should he do that? An oak is no perjurer.

STREPSIADES. I cannot tell, but it seems to me well argued. What is the thunder then?

SOCRATES. When a dry wind ascends to the Clouds and gets shut into them, it blows them out like a bladder; finally, being too confined, it bursts them, escapes with fierce violence and a roar to flash into flame by reason of its own impetuosity.

STREPSIADES. Forsooth, 'tis just what happened to me one day. 'Twas at the feast of Zeus! I was cooking a sow's belly for my family and I had forgotten to slit it open. It swelled out and, suddenly bursting, discharged itself right into my eyes and burnt my face.

CHORUS. Oh, mortal! you, who desire to instruct yourself in our great wisdom, the Athenians, the Greeks will envy you your good fortune. Only you must have the memory and ardour for study, you must know how to stand the tests, hold your own, go forward without feeling fatigue, caring but little for food, abstaining from wine, gymnastic exercises and other similar follies, in fact, you must believe as every man of intellect should, that the greatest of all blessings is to live and think more clearly than the vulgar herd, to shine in the contests of words.

STREPSIADES. If it be a question of hardiness for labour, of spending whole nights at work, of living sparingly, of fighting my stomach and only eating chick-pease, rest assured, I am as hard as an anvil.

SOCRATES. Henceforward, following our example, you will recognize no other gods but Chaos, the Clouds and the Tongue, these three alone.

STREPSIADES. I would not speak to the others, even if I should meet them in the street; not a single sacrifice, not a libation, not a grain of incense for them!

CHORUS. Tell us boldly then what you want of us; you cannot fail to succeed, if you honour and revere us and if you are resolved to become a clever man.

STREPSIADES. Oh, sovereign goddesses, 'tis but a very small favour that I ask of you; grant that I may distance all the Greeks by a hundred stadia in the art of speaking.

CHORUS. We grant you this, and henceforward no eloquence shall more often succeed with the people than your own.

STREPSIADES. May the god shield me from possessing great eloquence! 'Tis not what I want. I want to be able to turn bad lawsuits to my own advantage and to slip through the fingers of my creditors.

CHORUS. It shall be as you wish, for your ambitions are modest. Commit yourself fearlessly to our ministers, the sophists.

STREPSIADES. This will I do, for I trust in you. Moreover there is no drawing back, what with these cursed horses and this marriage, which has eaten up my vitals. So let them do with me as they will; I yield my body to them. Come blows, come hunger,

---

[155] These three men have already been referred to.

[156] A promontory of Attica (the modern Cape Colonna) about fifty miles from the Piraeus. Here stood a magnificent Temple, dedicated to Athené.

thirst, heat or cold, little matters it to me; they may flay me, if I only escape my debts, if only I win the reputation of being a bold rascal, a fine speaker, impudent, shameless, a braggart, and adept at stringing lies, an old stager at quibbles, a complete table of the laws, a thorough rattle, a fox to slip through any hole; supple as a leathern strap, slippery as an eel, an artful fellow, a blusterer, a villain; a knave with a hundred faces, cunning, intolerable, a gluttonous dog. With such epithets do I seek to be greeted; on these terms, they can treat me as they choose, and, if they wish, by Demeter! they can turn me into sausages and serve me up to the philosophers.

CHORUS. Here have we a bold and well-disposed pupil indeed. When we shall have taught you, your glory among the mortals will reach even to the skies.

STREPSIADES. Wherein will that profit me?

CHORUS. You will pass your whole life among us and will be the most envied of men.

STREPSIADES. Shall I really ever see such happiness?

CHORUS. Clients will be everlastingly besieging your door in crowds, burning to get at you, to explain their business to you and to consult you about their suits, which, in return for your ability, will bring you in great sums. But, Socrates, begin the lessons you want to teach this old man; rouse his mind, try the strength of his intelligence.

SOCRATES. Come, tell me the kind of mind you have; 'tis important I know this, that I may order my batteries against you in a new fashion.

STREPSIADES. Eh, what! in the name of the gods, are you purposing to assault me then?

SOCRATES. No. I only wish to ask you some questions. Have you any memory?

STREPSIADES. That depends: if anything is owed me, my memory is excellent, but if I owe, alas! I have none whatever.

SOCRATES. Have you a natural gift for speaking?

STREPSIADES. For speaking, no; for cheating, yes.

SOCRATES. How will you be able to learn then?

STREPSIADES. Very easily, have no fear.

SOCRATES. Thus, when I throw forth some philosophical thought anent things celestial, you will seize it in its very flight?

STREPSIADES. Then I am to snap up wisdom much as a dog snaps up a morsel?

SOCRATES. Oh! the ignoramus! the barbarian! I greatly fear, old man, 'twill be needful for me to have recourse to blows. Now, let me hear what you do when you are beaten.

STREPSIADES. I receive the blow, then wait a moment, take my witnesses and finally summon my assailant at law.

SOCRATES. Come, take off your cloak.

STREPSIADES. Have I robbed you of anything?

SOCRATES. No, but 'tis usual to enter the school without your cloak.

STREPSIADES. But I am not come here to look for stolen goods.

SOCRATES. Off with it, fool!

STREPSIADES. Tell me, if I prove thoroughly attentive and learn with zeal, which of your disciples shall I resemble, do you think?

SOCRATES. You will be the image of Chaerephon.

STREPSIADES. Ah! unhappy me! I shall then be but half alive?

SOCRATES. A truce to this chatter! follow me and no more of it.

STREPSIADES. First give me a honey-cake, for to descend down there sets me all a-tremble; meseems 'tis the cave of Trophonius.

SOCRATES. But get in with you! What reason have you for thus dallying at the door?

CHORUS. Good luck! you have courage; may you succeed, you, who, though already so advanced in years, wish to instruct your mind with new studies and practise it in wisdom!

CHORUS. [*Parabasis.*] Spectators! By Bacchus, whose servant I am, I will frankly tell you the truth. May I secure both victory and renown as certainly as I hold you for adept critics and as I regard this comedy as my best. I wished to give you the first view of a work, which had cost me much trouble, but I withdrew, unjustly beaten by unskilful rivals.[157] 'Tis you, oh, enlightened public, for whom I have prepared my piece, that I reproach with this. Nevertheless I shall never willingly cease to seek the approval of the discerning. I have not forgotten the day, when men, whom one is happy to have for an audience, received my 'Young Man' and my 'Debauchee'[158] with so much favour in this very place. Then as yet virgin, my Muse had not attained the legal age for maternity;[159] she had to expose her first-born for another to adopt, and it has since grown up under your generous patronage. Ever since you have as good as sworn me your faithful alliance. Thus, like Electra[160] of the poets, my comedy has come to seek you to-day, hoping again to encounter such enlightened spectators. As far away as she can discern her Orestes, she will be able to recognize him by his curly head. And note her modest demeanour! She has not sewn on a piece of hanging leather, thick and reddened at the end,[161] to cause laughter among the children; she does not rail at the bald, neither does she dance the cordax;[162] no old man is seen, who, while uttering his lines, batters his questioner with a stick to make his poor jests pass muster.[163] She does not rush upon the scene carrying a torch and screaming, 'La, la! la, la!' No, she relies upon herself and her verses.... My value is so well known, that I take no further pride in it. I do not seek to deceive you, by reproducing the same subjects two or three times; I always invent fresh themes to present before you, themes that have no relation to each other and that are all clever. I attacked Cleon[164] to his face and when he was all-powerful; but he has fallen, and now I have no desire to kick him when he is down. My rivals, on the contrary, once that this wretched Hyperbolus has given them the cue, have never ceased setting upon both him and his mother. First Eupolis presented his 'Maricas';[165] this was simply my 'Knights,' whom this plagiarist had clumsily furbished up again by adding to the piece an old drunken

---

[157] The opening portion of the parabasis belongs to a second edition of the 'Clouds.' Aristophanes had been defeated by Cratinus and Amipsias, whose pieces, called the 'Bottle' and 'Connus,' had been crowned in preference to the 'Clouds,' which, it is said, was not received any better at its second representation.

[158] Two characters introduced into the 'Daedalians' by Aristophanes in strong contrast to each other. Some fragments of this piece remain to us.

[159] It was only at the age of thirty, according to some, of forty, according to others, that a man could present a piece in his own name. The 'Daedalians' had appeared under the auspices of Cleonides and Chalistrates, whom we find again later as actors in Aristophanes' pieces.

[160] Allusion to the recognition of Orestes by Electra at her brother's tomb. (*See* the 'Choëphorae' of Aeschylus.)

[161] An image of the penis, drooping in this case, instead of standing, carried as a phallic emblem in the Dionysiac processions.

[162] A licentious dance.

[163] This coarse way of exciting laughter, says the scholiast, had been used by Eupolis, the comic writer, a rival of Aristophanes.

[164] In the 'Knights.'

[165] Presented in 421 B.C. The 'Clouds' having been played a second time in 419 B.C., one may conclude that this piece had appeared a third time on the Athenian stage.

woman, so that she might dance the cordax. 'Twas an old idea, taken from Phrynichus, who caused his old hag to be devoured by a monster of the deep.[166] Then Hermippus[167] fell foul of Hyperbolus and now all the others fall upon him and repeat my comparison of the eels. May those who find amusement in their pieces not be pleased with mine, but as for you, who love and applaud my inventions, why, posterity will praise your good taste.

Oh, ruler of Olympus, all-powerful king of the gods, great Zeus, it is thou whom I first invoke; protect this chorus; and thou too, Posidon, whose dread trident upheaves at the will of thy anger both the bowels of the earth and the salty waves of the ocean. I invoke my illustrious father, the divine Aether, the universal sustainer of life, and Phoebus, who, from the summit of his chariot, sets the world aflame with his dazzling rays, Phoebus, a mighty deity amongst the gods and adored amongst mortals.

Most wise spectators, lend us all your attention. Give heed to our just reproaches. There exist no gods to whom this city owes more than it does to us, whom alone you forget. Not a sacrifice, not a libation is there for those who protect you! Have you decreed some mad expedition? Well! we thunder or we fall down in rain. When you chose that enemy of heaven, the Paphlagonian tanner,[168] for a general, we knitted our brow, we caused our wrath to break out; the lightning shot forth, the thunder pealed, the moon deserted her course and the sun at once veiled his beam threatening no longer to give you light, if Cleon became general. Nevertheless you elected him; 'tis said, Athens never resolves upon some fatal step but the gods turn these errors into her greatest gain. Do you wish that this election should even now be a success for you? 'Tis a very simple thing to do; condemn this rapacious gull named Cleon[169] for bribery and extortion, fit a wooden collar tight round his neck, and your error will be rectified and the commonweal will at once regain its old prosperity.

Aid me also, Phoebus, god of Delos, who reignest on the cragged peaks of Cynthia;[170] and thou, happy virgin,[171] to whom the Lydian damsels offer pompous sacrifice in a temple of gold; and thou, goddess of our country, Athené, armed with the aegis, the protectress of Athens; and thou, who, surrounded by the Bacchanals of Delphi, roamest over the rocks of Parnassus shaking the flame of thy resinous torch, thou, Bacchus, the god of revel and joy.

As we were preparing to come here, we were hailed by the Moon and were charged to wish joy and happiness both to the Athenians and to their allies; further, she said that she was enraged and that you treated her very shamefully, her, who does not pay you in words alone, but who renders you all real benefits. Firstly, thanks to her, you save at least a drachma each month for lights, for each, as he is leaving home at night, says, "Slave, buy no torches, for the moonlight is beautiful,"—not to name a thousand other benefits. Nevertheless you do not reckon the days correctly and your calendar is naught but

---

[166] Doubtless a parody of the legend of Andromeda.
[167] A poet of the older comedy, who had written forty plays. It is said that he dared to accuse Aspasia, the mistress of Pericles, of impiety and the practice of prostitution.
[168] Cleon.
[169] This part of the parabasis belongs to the first edition of the 'Clouds,' since Aristophanes here speaks of Cleon as alive.
[170] A mountain in Delos, dedicated to Apollo and Diana.
[171] Artemis.

confusion.[172] Consequently the gods load her with threats each time they get home and are disappointed of their meal, because the festival has not been kept in the regular order of time. When you should be sacrificing, you are putting to the torture or administering justice. And often, we others, the gods, are fasting in token of mourning for the death of Memnon or Sarpedon,[173] while you are devoting yourselves to joyous libations. 'Tis for this, that last year, when the lot would have invested Hyperbolus[174] with the duty of Amphictyon, we took his crown from him, to teach him that time must be divided according to the phases of the moon.

SOCRATES. By Respiration, the Breath of Life! By Chaos! By the Air! I have never seen a man so gross, so inept, so stupid, so forgetful. All the little quibbles, which I teach him, he forgets even before he has learnt them. Yet I will not give it up, I will make him come out here into the open air. Where are you, Strepsiades? Come, bring your couch out here.

STREPSIADES. But the bugs will not allow me to bring it.

SOCRATES. Have done with such nonsense! place it there and pay attention.

STREPSIADES. Well, here I am.

SOCRATES. Good! Which science of all those you have never been taught, do you wish to learn first? The measures, the rhythms or the verses?

STREPSIADES. Why, the measures; the flour dealer cheated me out of two *choenixes* the other day.

SOCRATES. 'Tis not about that I ask you, but which, according to you, is the best measure, the trimeter or the tetrameter?[175]

STREPSIADES. The one I prefer is the semisextarius.

SOCRATES. You talk nonsense, my good fellow.

STREPSIADES. I will wager your tetrameter is the semisextarius.[176]

SOCRATES. Plague seize the dunce and the fool! Come, perchance you will learn the rhythms quicker.

STREPSIADES. Will the rhythms supply me with food?

SOCRATES. First they will help you to be pleasant in company, then to know what is meant by oenoplian rhythm[177] and what by the dactylic.[178]

---

[172] An allusion to the reform, which the astronomer Meton had wanted to introduce into the calendar. Cleostratus of Tenedos, at the beginning of the fifth century, had devised the *octaeteris*, or cycle of eight years, and this had been generally adopted. This is how this system arrived at an agreement between the solar and the lunar periods: 8 solar years containing 2922 days, while 8 lunar years only contain 2832 days, there was a difference of 90 days, for which Cleostratus compensated by intercalating 3 months of 30 days each, which were placed after the third, fifth and eighth year of the cycle. Hence these years had an extra month each. But in this system, the lunar months had been reckoned as 354 days, whereas they are really 354 days, 8 hours, 48 minutes. To rectify this minor error Meton invented a cycle of 19 years, which bears his name. This new system which he tried to introduce naturally caused some disturbance in the order of the festivals, and for this or some other reason his system was not adopted. The octaeteris continued to be used for all public purposes, the only correction being, that three extra days were added to every second octaeteris.

[173] Both sons of Zeus.

[174] Hyperbolus had supported Meton in his desire for reform. Having been sent as the Athenian deputy to the council of the Amphictyons, he should, like his colleagues, have returned to Athens with his head wreathed with laurel. It is said the wind took this from him; the Clouds boast of the achievement.

[175] These are poetical measures; Strepsiades thinks measures of capacity are meant.

[176] Containing four *choenixes*.

[177] So called from its stirring, warlike character; it was composed of two dactyls and a spondee, followed again by two dactyls and a spondee.

[178] Composed of dactyls and anapaests.

STREPSIADES. Of the dactyl? I know that quite well.

SOCRATES. What is it then?

STREPSIADES. Why, 'tis this finger; formerly, when a child, I used this one.[179]

SOCRATES. You are as low-minded as you are stupid.

STREPSIADES. But, wretched man, I do not want to learn all this.

SOCRATES. Then what *do* you want to know?

STREPSIADES. Not that, not that, but the art of false reasoning.

SOCRATES. But you must first learn other things. Come, what are the male quadrupeds?

STREPSIADES. Oh! I know the males thoroughly. Do you take me for a fool then? The ram, the buck, the bull, the dog, the pigeon.

SOCRATES. Do you see what you are doing; is not the female pigeon called the same as the male?

STREPSIADES. How else? Come now?

SOCRATES. How else? With you then 'tis pigeon and pigeon!

STREPSIADES. 'Tis true, by Posidon! but what names do you want me to give them?

SOCRATES. Term the female pigeonnette and the male pigeon.

STREPSIADES. Pigeonnette! hah! by the Air! That's splendid! for that lesson bring out your kneading-trough and I will fill him with flour to the brim.

SOCRATES. There you are wrong again; you make *trough* masculine and it should be feminine.

STREPSIADES. What? if I say *him*, do I make the *trough* masculine?

SOCRATES. Assuredly! would you not say him for Cleonymus?

STREPSIADES. Well?

SOCRATES. Then trough is of the same gender as Cleonymus?

STREPSIADES. Oh! good sir! Cleonymus never had a kneading-trough;[180] he used a round mortar for the purpose. But come, tell me what I *should* say?

SOCRATES. For trough you should say *her* as you would for Sostraté.[181]

STREPSIADES. *Her*?

SOCRATES. In this manner you make it truly female.

STREPSIADES. That's it! *Her* for trough and *her* for Cleonymus.[182]

SOCRATES. Now I must teach you to distinguish the masculine proper names from those that are feminine.

STREPSIADES. Ah! I know the female names well.

SOCRATES. Name some then.

STREPSIADES. Lysilla, Philinna, Clitagora, Demetria.

SOCRATES. And what are masculine names?

STREPSIADES. They are countless—Philoxenus, Melesias, Amynias.

SOCRATES. But, wretched man, the last two are not masculine.

STREPSIADES. You do not reckon them masculine?

SOCRATES. Not at all. If you met Amynias, how would you hail him?

STREPSIADES. How? Why, I should shout, "Hi! hither, Amynia!"[183]

---

[179] [Greek: *Daktylos*] means, of course, both *dactyl*, name of a metrical foot, and finger. Strepsiades presents his middle finger, with the other fingers and thumb bent under in an indecent gesture meant to suggest the penis and testicles. The Romans for this reason called the middle finger 'digitus infamis,' the *unseemly finger*. The Emperor Nero is said to have offered his hand to courtiers to kiss sometimes in this indecent way.

[180] Meaning he was too poor, Aristophanes represents him as a glutton and a parasite.

[181] A woman's name.

[182] He is classed as a woman because of his cowardice and effeminacy.

SOCRATES. Do you see? 'tis a female name that you give him.

STREPSIADES. And is it not rightly done, since he refuses military service? But what use is there in learning what we all know?

SOCRATES. You know nothing about it. Come, lie down there.

STREPSIADES. What for?

SOCRATES. Ponder awhile over matters that interest you.

STREPSIADES. Oh! I pray you, not there! but, if I must lie down and ponder, let me lie on the ground.

SOCRATES. 'Tis out of the question. Come! on to the couch!

STREPSIADES. What cruel fate! What a torture the bugs will this day put me to!

SOCRATES. Ponder and examine closely, gather your thoughts together, let your mind turn to every side of things; if you meet with a difficulty, spring quickly to some other idea; above all, keep your eyes away from all gentle sleep.

STREPSIADES. Oh, woe, woe! oh, woe, woe!

SOCRATES. What ails you? why do you cry so?

STREPSIADES. Oh! I am a dead man! Here are these cursed Corinthians[184] advancing upon me from all corners of the couch; they are biting me, they are gnawing at my sides, they are drinking all my blood, they are twitching off my testicles, they are exploring all up my back, they are killing me!

SOCRATES. Not so much wailing and clamour, if you please.

STREPSIADES. How can I obey? I have lost my money and my complexion, my blood and my slippers, and to cap my misery, I must keep awake on this couch, when scarce a breath of life is left in me.

SOCRATES. Well now! what are you doing? are you reflecting?

STREPSIADES. Yes, by Posidon!

SOCRATES. What about?

STREPSIADES. Whether the bugs will not entirely devour me.

SOCRATES. May death seize you, accursed man!

STREPSIADES. Ah! it has already.

SOCRATES. Come, no giving way! Cover up your head; the thing to do is to find an ingenious alternative.

STREPSIADES. An alternative! ah! I only wish one would come to me from within these coverlets!

SOCRATES. Hold! let us see what our fellow is doing. Ho! you! are you asleep?

STREPSIADES. No, by Apollo!

SOCRATES. Have you got hold of anything?

STREPSIADES. No, nothing whatever.

SOCRATES. Nothing at all!

STREPSIADES. No, nothing but my tool, which I've got in my hand.

SOCRATES. Are you not going to cover your head immediately and ponder?

STREPSIADES. Over what? Come, Socrates, tell me.

SOCRATES. Think first what you want, and then tell me.

STREPSIADES. But I have told you a thousand times what I want. 'Tis not to pay any of my creditors.

SOCRATES. Come, wrap yourself up; concentrate your mind, which wanders too lightly,

---

[183] In Greek, the vocative of Amynias is Amynia; thus it has a feminine termination.

[184] The Corinthians, the allies of Sparta, ravaged Attica. [Greek: Kor], the first portion of the Greek word, is the root of the word which means a bug in the same language.

study every detail, scheme and examine thoroughly.

STREPSIADES. Oh, woe! woe! oh dear! oh dear!

SOCRATES. Keep yourself quiet, and if any notion troubles you, put it quickly aside, then resume it and think over it again.

STREPSIADES. My dear little Socrates!

SOCRATES. What is it, old greybeard?

STREPSIADES. I have a scheme for not paying my debts.

SOCRATES. Let us hear it.

STREPSIADES. Tell me, if I purchased a Thessalian witch, I could make the moon descend during the night and shut it, like a mirror, into a round box and there keep it carefully....

SOCRATES. How would you gain by that?

STREPSIADES. How? Why, if the moon did not rise, I would have no interest to pay.

SOCRATES. Why so?

STREPSIADES. Because money is lent by the month.

SOCRATES. Good! but I am going to propose another trick to you. If you were condemned to pay five talents, how would you manage to quash that verdict? Tell me.

STREPSIADES. How? how? I don't know, I must think.

SOCRATES. Do you always shut your thoughts within yourself. Let your ideas fly in the air, like a may-bug, tied by the foot with a thread.

STREPSIADES. I have found a very clever way to annul that conviction; you will admit that much yourself.

SOCRATES. What is it?

STREPSIADES. Have you ever seen a beautiful, transparent stone at the druggists, with which you may kindle fire?

SOCRATES. You mean a crystal lens.[185]

STREPSIADES. Yes.

SOCRATES. Well, what then?

STREPSIADES. If I placed myself with this stone in the sun and a long way off from the clerk, while he was writing out the conviction, I could make all the wax, upon which the words were written, melt.

SOCRATES. Well thought out, by the Graces!

STREPSIADES. Ah! I am delighted to have annulled the decree that was to cost me five talents.

SOCRATES. Come, take up this next question quickly.

STREPSIADES. Which?

SOCRATES. If, when summoned to court, you were in danger of losing your case for want of witnesses, how would you make the conviction fall upon your opponent?

STREPSIADES. 'Tis very simple and most easy.

SOCRATES. Let me hear.

STREPSIADES. This way. If another case had to be pleaded before mine was called, I should run and hang myself.

SOCRATES. You talk rubbish!

STREPSIADES. Not so, by the gods! if I was dead, no action could lie against me.

---

[185] Mirrors, or burning glasses, are meant, such as those used by Archimedes two centuries later at the siege of Syracuse, when he set the Roman fleet on fire from the walls of the city.

SOCRATES. You are merely beating the air. Begone! I will give you no more lessons.

STREPSIADES. Why not? Oh! Socrates! in the name of the gods!

SOCRATES. But you forget as fast as you learn. Come, what was the thing I taught you first? Tell me.

STREPSIADES. Ah! let me see. What was the first thing? What was it then? Ah! that thing in which we knead the bread, oh! my god! what do you call it?

SOCRATES. Plague take the most forgetful and silliest of old addlepates!

STREPSIADES. Alas! what a calamity! what will become of me? I am undone if I do not learn how to ply my tongue. Oh! Clouds! give me good advice.

CHORUS. Old man, we counsel you, if you have brought up a son, to send him to learn in your stead.

STREPSIADES. Undoubtedly I have a son, as well endowed as the best, but he is unwilling to learn. What will become of me?

CHORUS. And you don't make him obey you?

STREPSIADES. You see, he is big and strong; moreover, through his mother he is a descendant of those fine birds, the race of Coesyra.[186] Nevertheless, I will go and find him, and if he refuses, I will turn him out of the house. Go in, Socrates, and wait for me awhile.

CHORUS. [to SOCRATES.] Do you understand, that, thanks to us, you will be loaded with benefits? Here is a man, ready to obey you in all things. You see how he is carried away with admiration and enthusiasm. Profit by it to clip him as short as possible; fine chances are all too quickly gone.

STREPSIADES. No, by the Clouds! you stay no longer here; go and devour the ruins of your uncle Megacles' fortune.

PHIDIPPIDES. Oh! my poor father! what has happened to you? By the Olympian Zeus! you are no longer in your senses!

STREPSIADES. See! see! "the Olympian Zeus." Oh! the fool! to believe in Zeus at your age!

PHIDIPPIDES. What is there in that to make you laugh?

STREPSIADES. You are then a tiny little child, if you credit such antiquated rubbish! But come here, that I may teach you; I will tell you something very necessary to know to be a man; but you will not repeat it to anybody.

PHIDIPPIDES. Come, what is it?

STREPSIADES. Just now you swore by Zeus.

PHIDIPPIDES. Aye, that I did.

STREPSIADES. Do you see how good it is to learn? Phidippides, there is no Zeus.

PHIDIPPIDES. What is there then?

STREPSIADES. 'Tis the Whirlwind, that has driven out Jupiter and is King now.

PHIDIPPIDES. Go to! what drivel!

STREPSIADES. Know it to be the truth.

PHIDIPPIDES. And who says so?

STREPSIADES. 'Tis Socrates, the Melian,[187] and Chaerephon, who knows how to measure the jump of a flea.

PHIDIPPIDES. Have you reached such a pitch of madness that you believe those bilious fellows?

---

[186] That is, the family of the Alcmaeonidae; Coesyra was wife of Alcmaeon.

[187] Socrates was an Athenian; but the atheist Diagoras, known as 'the enemy of the gods' hailed from the island of Melos. Strepsiades, crediting Socrates with the same incredulity, assigns him the same birthplace.

STREPSIADES. Use better language, and do not insult men who are clever and full of wisdom, who, to economize, are never shaved, shun the gymnasia and never go to the baths, while you, you only await my death to eat up my wealth. But come, come as quickly as you can to learn in my stead.

PHIDIPPIDES. And what good can be learnt of them?

STREPSIADES. What good indeed? Why, all human knowledge. Firstly, you will know yourself grossly ignorant. But await me here awhile.

PHIDIPPIDES. Alas! what is to be done? My father has lost his wits. Must I have him certificated for lunacy, or must I order his coffin?

STREPSIADES. Come! what kind of bird is this? tell me.

PHIDIPPIDES. A pigeon.

STREPSIADES. Good! And this female?

PHIDIPPIDES. A pigeon.

STREPSIADES. The same for both? You make me laugh! For the future you will call this one a pigeonnette and the other a pigeon.

PHIDIPPIDES. A pigeonnette! These then are the fine things you have just learnt at the school of these sons of the Earth![188]

STREPSIADES. And many others; but what I learnt I forgot at once, because I am too old.

PHIDIPPIDES. So this is why you have lost your cloak?

STREPSIADES. I have not lost it, I have consecrated it to Philosophy.

PHIDIPPIDES. And what have you done with your sandals, you poor fool?

STREPSIADES. If I have lost them, it is for what was necessary, just as Pericles did.[189] But come, move yourself, let us go in; if necessary, do wrong to obey your father. When you were six years old and still lisped, 'twas I who obeyed you. I remember at the feasts of Zeus you had a consuming wish for a little chariot and I bought it for you with the first obolus which I received as a juryman in the Courts.

PHIDIPPIDES. You will soon repent of what you ask me to do.

STREPSIADES. Oh! now I am happy! He obeys. Here, Socrates, here! Come out quick! Here I am bringing you my son; he refused, but I have persuaded him.

SOCRATES. Why, he is but a child yet. He is not used to these baskets, in which we suspend our minds.[190]

PHIDIPPIDES. To make you better used to them, I would you were hung.

STREPSIADES. A curse upon you! you insult your master!

SOCRATES. "I would you were hung!" What a stupid speech! and so emphatically spoken! How can one ever get out of an accusation with such a tone, summon witnesses or touch or convince? And yet when we think, Hyperbolus learnt all this for one talent!

---

[188] *i.e.* the enemies of the gods. An allusion to the giants, the sons of Earth, who had endeavoured to scale heaven.

[189] Pericles had squandered all the wealth accumulated in the Acropolis upon the War. When he handed in his accounts, he refused to explain the use of a certain twenty talents and simply said, "*I spent them on what was necessary.*" Upon hearing of this reply, the Lacedaemonians, who were already discontented with their kings, Cleandrides and Plistoanax, whom they accused of carrying on the war in Attica with laxness, exiled the first-named and condemned the second to payment of a fine of fifteen talents for treachery. In fact, the Spartans were convinced that Pericles had kept silent as to what he had done with the twenty talents, because he did not want to say openly, "*I gave this sum to the Kings of Lacedaemon.*"

[190] The basket in which Aristophanes shows us Socrates suspended to bring his mind nearer to the subtle regions of air.

STREPSIADES. Rest undisturbed and teach him. 'Tis a most intelligent nature. Even when quite little he amused himself at home with making houses, carving boats, constructing little chariots of leather, and understood wonderfully how to make frogs out of pomegranate rinds. Teach him both methods of reasoning, the strong and also the weak, which by false arguments triumphs over the strong; if not the two, at least the false, and that in every possible way.

SOCRATES. 'Tis Just and Unjust Discourse themselves that shall instruct him.[191]

STREPSIADES. I go, but forget it not, he must always, always be able to confound the true.

JUST DISCOURSE. Come here! Shameless as you may be, will you dare to show your face to the spectators?

UNJUST DISCOURSE. Take me where you list. I seek a throng, so that I may the better annihilate you.

JUST DISCOURSE. Annihilate me! Do you forget who you are?

UNJUST DISCOURSE. I am Reasoning.

JUST DISCOURSE. Yes, the weaker Reasoning.[192]

UNJUST DISCOURSE. But I triumph over you, who claim to be the stronger.

JUST DISCOURSE. By what cunning shifts, pray?

UNJUST DISCOURSE. By the invention of new maxims.

JUST DISCOURSE. ... which are received with favour by these fools.

UNJUST DISCOURSE. Say rather, by these wiseacres.

JUST DISCOURSE. I am going to destroy you mercilessly.

UNJUST DISCOURSE. How pray? Let us see you do it.

JUST DISCOURSE. By saying what is true.

UNJUST DISCOURSE. I shall retort and shall very soon have the better of you. First, I maintain that justice has no existence.

JUST DISCOURSE. Has no existence?

UNJUST DISCOURSE. No existence! Why, where are they?

JUST DISCOURSE. With the gods.

UNJUST DISCOURSE. How then, if justice exists, was Zeus not put to death for having put his father in chains?

JUST DISCOURSE. Bah! this is enough to turn my stomach! A basin, quick!

UNJUST DISCOURSE. You are an old driveller and stupid withal.

JUST DISCOURSE. And you a debauchee and a shameless fellow.

UNJUST DISCOURSE. Hah! What sweet expressions!

JUST DISCOURSE. An impious buffoon!

UNJUST DISCOURSE. You crown me with roses and with lilies.

JUST DISCOURSE. A parricide.

UNJUST DISCOURSE. Why, you shower gold upon me.

JUST DISCOURSE. Formerly, 'twas a hailstorm of blows.

UNJUST DISCOURSE. I deck myself with your abuse.

JUST DISCOURSE. What impudence!

UNJUST DISCOURSE. What tomfoolery!

---

[191] The scholiast tells us that Just Discourse and Unjust Discourse were brought upon the stage in cages, like cocks that are going to fight. Perhaps they were even dressed up as cocks, or at all events wore cocks' heads as their masks.

[192] In the language of the schools of philosophy just reasoning was called 'the stronger'—[Greek: *ho kreitton logos*], unjust reasoning, 'the weaker'—[Greek: *ho hetton logos*.]

JUST DISCOURSE. 'Tis because of you that the youth no longer attends the schools. The Athenians will soon recognize what lessons you teach those who are fools enough to believe you.

UNJUST DISCOURSE. You are overwhelmed with wretchedness.

JUST DISCOURSE. And you, you prosper. Yet you were poor when you said, "I am the Mysian Telephus,"[193] and used to stuff your wallet with maxims of Pandeletus[194] to nibble at.

UNJUST DISCOURSE. Oh! the beautiful wisdom, of which you are now boasting!

JUST DISCOURSE. Madman! But yet madder the city that keeps you, you, the corrupter of its youth!

UNJUST DISCOURSE. 'Tis not you who will teach this young man; you are as old and out of date as Saturn.

JUST DISCOURSE. Nay, it will certainly be I, if he does not wish to be lost and to practise verbosity only.

UNJUST DISCOURSE. [to PHIDIPPIDES.] Come hither and leave him to beat the air.

JUST DISCOURSE. [to UNJUST DISCOURSE.] Evil be unto you, if you touch him.

CHORUS. A truce to your quarrellings and abuse! But expound, you, what you taught us formerly, and you, your new doctrine. Thus, after hearing each of you argue, he will be able to choose betwixt the two schools.

JUST DISCOURSE. I am quite agreeable.

UNJUST DISCOURSE. And I too.

CHORUS. Who is to speak first?

UNJUST DISCOURSE. Let it be my opponent, he has my full consent; then I will follow upon the very ground he shall have chosen and shall shatter him with a hail of new ideas and subtle fancies; if after that he dares to breathe another word, I shall sting him in the face and in the eyes with our maxims, which are as keen as the sting of a wasp, and he will die.

CHORUS. Here are two rivals confident in their powers of oratory and in the thoughts over which they have pondered so long. Let us see which will come triumphant out of the contest. This wisdom, for which my friends maintain such a persistent fight, is in great danger. Come then, you, who crowned men of other days with so many virtues, plead the cause dear to you, make yourself known to us.

JUST DISCOURSE. Very well, I will tell you what was the old education, when I used to teach justice with so much success and when modesty was held in veneration. Firstly, it was required of a child, that it should not utter a word. In the street, when they went to the music-school, all the youths of the same district marched lightly clad and ranged in good order, even when the snow was falling in great flakes. At the master's house they had to stand, their legs apart, and they were taught to sing either, "Pallas, the Terrible, who overturneth cities," or "A noise resounded from afar"[195] in the solemn tones of the ancient harmony. If anyone indulged in buffoonery or lent his voice any of the soft inflexions, like those which to-day the disciples of

---

[193] A character in one of the tragedies of Aeschylus, a beggar and a clever, plausible speaker.

[194] A sycophant and a quibbler, renowned for his unparalleled bad faith in the law-suits he was perpetually bringing forward.

[195] The opening words of two hymns, attributed to Lamprocles, an ancient lyric poet, the son or the pupil of Medon.

Phrynis[196] take so much pains to form, he was treated as an enemy of the Muses and belaboured with blows. In the wrestling school they would sit with outstretched legs and without display of any indecency to the curious. When they rose, they would smooth over the sand, so as to leave no trace to excite obscene thoughts. Never was a child rubbed with oil below the belt; the rest of their bodies thus retained its fresh bloom and down, like a velvety peach. They were not to be seen approaching a lover and themselves rousing his passion by soft modulation of the voice and lustful gaze. At table, they would not have dared, before those older than themselves, to have taken a radish, an aniseed or a leaf of parsley, and much less eat fish or thrushes or cross their legs.

UNJUST DISCOURSE. What antiquated rubbish! Have we got back to the days of the festivals of Zeus Polieus,[197] to the Buphonia, to the time of the poet Cecydes[198] and the golden cicadas?[199]

JUST DISCOURSE. 'Tis nevertheless by suchlike teaching I built up the men of Marathon. But you, you teach the children of to-day to bundle themselves quickly into their clothes, and I am enraged when I see them at the Panathenaea forgetting Athené while they dance, and covering themselves with their bucklers. Hence, young man, dare to range yourself beside me, who follow justice and truth; you will then be able to shun the public place, to refrain from the baths, to blush at all that is shameful, to fire up if your virtue is mocked at, to give place to your elders, to honour your parents, in short, to avoid all that is evil. Be modesty itself, and do not run to applaud the dancing girls; if you delight in such scenes, some courtesan will cast you her apple and your reputation will be done for. Do not bandy words with your father, nor treat him as a dotard, nor reproach the old man, who has cherished you, with his age.

UNJUST DISCOURSE. If you listen to him, by Bacchus! you will be the image of the sons of Hippocrates[200] and will be called *mother's great ninny*.

JUST DISCOURSE. No, but you will pass your days at the gymnasia, glowing with strength and health; you will not go to the public place to cackle and wrangle as is done nowadays; you will not live in fear that you may be dragged before the courts for some trifle exaggerated by quibbling. But you will go down to the Academy[201] to run beneath the sacred olives with some virtuous friend of your own age, your head encircled with the white reed, enjoying your ease and breathing the perfume of the yew and of the fresh sprouts of the poplar, rejoicing in the return of springtide and gladly listening to the gentle rustle of the plane-tree and the elm. If you devote yourself to practising my precepts, your chest will be stout, your colour glowing,

---

[196] A poet and musician of Mitylené, who gained the prize of the lyre at the Panathenaea in 457 B.C. He lived at the Court of Hiero, where, Suidas says, he was at first a slave and the cook. He added two strings to the lyre, which hitherto had had only seven. He composed effeminate airs of a style unknown before his day.

[197] Zeus had a temple in the citadel of Athens under the name of Polieus or protector of the city; bullocks were sacrificed to him (Buphonia). In the days of Aristophanes, these feasts had become neglected.

[198] One of the oldest of the dithyrambic poets.

[199] Used by the ancient Athenians to keep their hair in place. The custom was said to have a threefold significance; by it the Athenians wanted to show that they were musicians, autochthons (*i.e.* indigenous to the country) and worshippers of Apollo. Indeed, grasshoppers were considered to sing with harmony; they swarmed on Attic soil and were sacred to Phoebus, the god of music.

[200] Telesippus, Demophon and Pericles by name; they were a byword at Athens for their stupidity. Hippocrates was a general.

[201] The famous gardens of the Academia, just outside the walls of Athens; they included gymnasia, lecture halls, libraries and picture galleries. Near by was a wood of sacred olives.

your shoulders broad, your tongue short, your hips muscular, but your penis small. But if you follow the fashions of the day, you will be pallid in hue, have narrow shoulders, a narrow chest, a long tongue, small hips and a big tool; you will know how to spin forth long-winded arguments on law. You will be persuaded also to regard as splendid everything that is shameful and as shameful everything that is honourable; in a word, you will wallow in debauchery like Antimachus.[202]

CHORUS. How beautiful, high-souled, brilliant is this wisdom that you practise! What a sweet odour of honesty is emitted by your discourse! Happy were those men of other days who lived when you were honoured! And you, seductive talker, come, find some fresh arguments, for your rival has done wonders. Bring out against him all the battery of your wit, if you desire to beat him and not to be laughed out of court.

UNJUST DISCOURSE. At last! I was choking with impatience, I was burning to upset all his arguments! If I am called the Weaker Reasoning in the schools, 'tis precisely because I was the first before all others to discover the means to confute the laws and the decrees of justice. To invoke solely the weaker arguments and yet triumph is a talent worth more than a hundred thousand drachmae. But see how I shall batter down the sort of education of which he is so proud. Firstly, he forbids you to bathe in hot water. What grounds have you for condemning hot baths?

JUST DISCOURSE. Because they are baneful and enervate men.

UNJUST DISCOURSE. Enough said! Oh! you poor wrestler! From the very outset I have seized you and hold you round the middle; you cannot escape me. Tell me, of all the sons of Zeus, who had the stoutest heart, who performed the most doughty deeds?

JUST DISCOURSE. None, in my opinion, surpassed Heracles.

UNJUST DISCOURSE. Where have you ever seen cold baths called 'Baths of Heracles'?[203] And yet who was braver than he?

JUST DISCOURSE. 'Tis because of such quibbles, that the baths are seen crowded with young folk, who chatter there the livelong day while the gymnasia remain empty.

UNJUST DISCOURSE. Next you condemn the habit of frequenting the market-place, while I approve this. If it were wrong Homer would never have made Nestor[204] speak in public as well as all his wise heroes. As for the art of speaking, he tells you, young men should not practise it; I hold the contrary. Furthermore he preaches chastity to them. Both precepts are equally harmful. Have you ever seen chastity of any use to anyone? Answer and try to confute me.

JUST DISCOURSE. To many; for instance, Peleus won a sword thereby.[205]

UNJUST DISCOURSE. A sword! Ah! what a fine present to make him! Poor wretch! Hyperbolus, the lamp-seller, thanks to his villainy, has gained more than ... I do not know how many talents, but certainly no sword.

---

[202] Apparently the historian of that name is meant; in any case it cannot refer to the celebrated epic poet, author of the 'Thebaïs.'

[203] Among the Greeks, hot springs bore the generic name of 'Baths of Heracles.' A legend existed that these had gushed forth spontaneously beneath the tread of the hero, who would plunge into them and there regain fresh strength to continue his labours.

[204] King of Pylos, according to Homer, the wisest of all the Greeks.

[205] Peleus, son of Aeacus, having resisted the appeals of Astydamia, the wife of Acastus, King of Iolchos, was denounced to her husband by her as having wished to seduce her, so that she might be avenged for his disdain. Acastus in his anger took Peleus to hunt with him on Mount Pelion, there deprived him of his weapons and left him a prey to wild animals. He was about to die, when Hermes brought him a sword forged by Hephaestus.

JUST DISCOURSE. Peleus owed it to his chastity that he became the husband of Thetis.[206]

UNJUST DISCOURSE. ... who left him in the lurch, for he was not the most ardent; in those nocturnal sports between two sheets, which so please women, he possessed but little merit. Get you gone, you are but an old fool. But you, young man, just consider a little what this temperance means and the delights of which it deprives you—young fellows, women, play, dainty dishes, wine, boisterous laughter. And what is life worth without these? Then, if you happen to commit one of these faults inherent in human weakness, some seduction or adultery, and you are caught in the act, you are lost, if you cannot speak. But follow my teaching and you will be able to satisfy your passions, to dance, to laugh, to blush at nothing. Are you surprised in adultery? Then up and tell the husband you are not guilty, and recall to him the example of Zeus, who allowed himself to be conquered by love and by women. Being but a mortal, can you be stronger than a god?

JUST DISCOURSE. And if your pupil gets impaled, his hairs plucked out, and he is seared with a hot ember,[207] how are you going to prove to him that he is not a filthy debauchee?

UNJUST DISCOURSE. And wherein lies the harm of being so?

JUST DISCOURSE. Is there anything worse than to have such a character?

UNJUST DISCOURSE. Now what will you say, if I beat you even on this point?

JUST DISCOURSE. I should certainly have to be silent then.

UNJUST DISCOURSE. Well then, reply! Our advocates, what are they?

JUST DISCOURSE. Low scum.

UNJUST DISCOURSE. Nothing is more true. And our tragic poets?

JUST DISCOURSE. Low scum.

UNJUST DISCOURSE. Well said again. And our demagogues?

JUST DISCOURSE. Low scum.

UNJUST DISCOURSE. You admit that you have spoken nonsense. And the spectators, what are they for the most part? Look at them.

JUST DISCOURSE. I am looking at them.

UNJUST DISCOURSE. Well! What do you see?

JUST DISCOURSE. By the gods, they are nearly all low scum. See, this one I know to be such and that one and that other with the long hair.

UNJUST DISCOURSE. What have you to say, then?

JUST DISCOURSE. I am beaten. Debauchees! in the name of the gods, receive my cloak;[208] I pass over to your ranks.

SOCRATES. Well then! do you take away your son or do you wish me to teach him how to speak?

STREPSIADES. Teach him, chastise him and do not fail to sharpen his tongue well, on one side for petty law-suits and on the other for important cases.

SOCRATES. Make yourself easy, I shall return to you an accomplished sophist.

---

[206] Thetis, to escape the solicitations of Peleus, assumed in turn the form of a bird, of a tree, and finally of a tigress; but Peleus learnt of Proteus the way of compelling Thetis to yield to his wishes. The gods were present at his nuptials and made the pair rich presents.

[207] According to the scholiast, an adulterer was punished in the following manner: a radish was forced up his rectum, then every hair was torn out round that region, and the portion so treated was then covered with burning embers.

[208] Having said this, Just Discourse threw his cloak into the amphitheatre and took a seat with the spectators.

PHIDIPPIDES. Very pale then and thoroughly hang-dog-looking.

STREPSIADES. Take him with you.

PHIDIPPIDES. I do assure you, you will repent it.

CHORUS. Judges, we are all about to tell you what you will gain by awarding us the crown as equity requires of you. In spring, when you wish to give your fields the first dressing, we will rain upon you first; the others shall wait. Then we will watch over your corn and over your vine-stocks; they will have no excess to fear, neither of heat nor of wet. But if a mortal dares to insult the goddesses of the Clouds, let him think of the ills we shall pour upon him. For him neither wine nor any harvest at all! Our terrible slings will mow down his young olive plants and his vines. If he is making bricks, it will rain, and our round hailstones will break the tiles of his roof. If he himself marries or any of his relations or friends, we shall cause rain to fall the whole night long. Verily, he would prefer to live in Egypt[209] than to have given this iniquitous verdict.

STREPSIADES. Another four, three, two days, then the eve, then the day, the fatal day of payment! I tremble, I quake, I shudder, for 'tis the day of the old moon and the new.[210] Then all my creditors take the oath, pay their deposits,[211] swear my downfall and my ruin. As for me, I beseech them to be reasonable, to be just, "My friend, do not demand this sum, wait a little for this other and give me time for this third one." Then they will pretend that at this rate they will never be repaid, will accuse me of bad faith and will threaten me with the law. Well then, let them sue me! I care nothing for that, if only Phidippides has learnt to speak fluently. I go to find out, let me knock at the door of the school.... Ho! slave, slave!

SOCRATES. Welcome! Strepsiades!

STREPSIADES. Welcome! Socrates! But first take this sack [*offers him a sack of flour;*] it is right to reward the master with some present. And my son, whom you took off lately, has he learnt this famous reasoning, tell me.

SOCRATES. He has learnt it.

STREPSIADES. What a good thing! Oh! thou divine Knavery!

SOCRATES. You will win just as many causes as you choose.

STREPSIADES. Even if I have borrowed before witnesses?

SOCRATES. So much the better, even if there are a thousand of 'em!

STREPSIADES. Then I am going to shout with all my might. "Woe to the usurers, woe to their capital and their interest and their compound interest! You shall play me no more bad turns. My son is being taught there, his tongue is being sharpened into a double-edged weapon; he is my defender, the saviour of my house, the ruin of my foes! His poor father was crushed down with misfortune and he delivers him." Go and call him to me quickly. Oh! my child! my dear little one! run forward to your father's voice!

SOCRATES. Here he is.

STREPSIADES. Oh, my friend, my dearest friend!

SOCRATES. Take your son, and get you gone.

STREPSIADES. Oh, my son! oh! oh! what a pleasure to see your pallor! You are ready first to deny and then to contradict; 'tis as clear as noon. What a child of your country

---

[209] Because it never rains there; for all other reasons residence in Egypt was looked upon as undesirable.

[210] That is, the last day of the month.

[211] By Athenian law, if anyone summoned another to appear before the Courts, he was obliged to deposit a sum sufficient to cover the costs of procedure.

you are! How your lips quiver with the famous, "What have you to say now?" How well you know, I am certain, to put on the look of a victim, when it is you who are making both victims and dupes! and what a truly Attic glance! Come, 'tis for you to save me, seeing it is you who have ruined me.

PHIDIPPIDES. What is it you fear then?

STREPSIADES. The day of the old and the new.

PHIDIPPIDES. Is there then a day of the old and the new?

STREPSIADES. The day on which they threaten to pay deposit against me.

PHIDIPPIDES. Then so much the worse for those who have deposited! for 'tis not possible for one day to be two.

STREPSIADES. What?

PHIDIPPIDES. Why, undoubtedly, unless a woman can be both old and young at the same time.

STREPSIADES. But so runs the law.

PHIDIPPIDES. I think the meaning of the law is quite misunderstood.

STREPSIADES. What does it mean?

PHIDIPPIDES. Old Solon loved the people.

STREPSIADES. What has that to do with the old day and the new?

PHIDIPPIDES. He has fixed two days for the summons, the last day of the old moon and the first day of the new; but the deposits must only be paid on the first day of the new moon.

STREPSIADES. And why did he also name the last day of the old?

PHIDIPPIDES. So, my dear sir, that the debtors, being there the day before, might free themselves by mutual agreement, or that else, if not, the creditor might begin his action on the morning of the new moon.

STREPSIADES. Why then do the magistrates have the deposits paid on the last of the month and not the next day?

PHIDIPPIDES. I think they do as the gluttons do, who are the first to pounce upon the dishes. Being eager to carry off these deposits, they have them paid in a day too soon.

STREPSIADES. Splendid! Ah! poor brutes,[212] who serve for food to us clever folk! You are only down here to swell the number, true blockheads, sheep for shearing, heap of empty pots! Hence I will sound the note of victory for my son and myself. "Oh! happy, Strepsiades! what cleverness is thine! and what a son thou hast here!" Thus my friends and my neighbours will say, jealous at seeing me gain all my suits. But come in, I wish to regale you first.

PASIAS. [to HIS WITNESS.] A man should never lend a single obolus. 'Twould be better to put on a brazen face at the outset than to get entangled in such matters. I want to see my money again and I bring you here to-day to attest the loan. I am going to make a foe of a neighbour; but, as long as I live, I do not wish my country to have to blush for me. Come, I am going to summon Strepsiades.

STREPSIADES. Who is this?

PASIAS. ... for the old day and the new.

STREPSIADES. I call you to witness, that he has named two days. What do you want of me?

---

[212] He points to an earthenware sphere, placed at the entrance of Socrates' dwelling, and which was intended to represent the Whirlwind, the deity of the philosophers. This sphere took the place of the column which the Athenians generally dedicated to Apollo, and which stood in the vestibule of their houses.

PASIAS. I claim of you the twelve minae, which you borrowed from me to buy the dapple-grey horse.

STREPSIADES. A horse! do you hear him? I, who detest horses, as is well known.

PASIAS. I call Zeus to witness, that you swore by the gods to return them to me.

STREPSIADES. Because at that time, by Zeus! Phidippides did not yet know the irrefutable argument.

PASIAS. Would you deny the debt on that account?

STREPSIADES. If not, what use is his science to me?

PASIAS. Will you dare to swear by the gods that you owe me nothing?

STREPSIADES. By which gods?

PASIAS. By Zeus, Hermes and Posidon!

STREPSIADES. Why, I would give three obols for the pleasure of swearing by them.

PASIAS. Woe upon you, impudent knave!

STREPSIADES. Oh! what a fine wine-skin you would make if flayed!

PASIAS. Heaven! he jeers at me!

STREPSIADES. It would hold six gallons easily.

PASIAS. By great Zeus! by all the gods! you shall not scoff at me with impunity.

STREPSIADES. Ah! how you amuse me with your gods! how ridiculous it seems to a sage to hear Zeus invoked.

PASIAS. Your blasphemies will one day meet their reward. But, come, will you repay me my money, yes or no? Answer me, that I may go.

STREPSIADES. Wait a moment, I am going to give you a distinct answer. [*Goes indoors and returns immediately with a kneading-trough.*]

PASIAS. What do you think he will do?

WITNESS. He will pay the debt.

STREPSIADES. Where is the man who demands money? Tell me, what is this?

PASIAS. Him? Why he is your kneading-trough.

STREPSIADES. And you dare to demand money of me, when you are so ignorant? I will not return an obolus to anyone who says *him* instead of *her* for a kneading-trough.

PASIAS. You will not repay?

STREPSIADES. Not if I know it. Come, an end to this, pack off as quick as you can.

PASIAS. I go, but, may I die, if it be not to pay my deposit for a summons.

STREPSIADES. Very well! 'Twill be so much more to the bad to add to the twelve minae. But truly it makes me sad, for I do pity a poor simpleton who says *him* for a kneading-trough.

AMYNIAS. Woe! ah woe is me!

STREPSIADES. Hold! who is this whining fellow? Can it be one of the gods of Carcinus?[213]

AMYNIAS. Do you want to know who I am? I am a man of misfortune!

STREPSIADES. Get on your way then.

AMYNIAS. Oh! cruel god! Oh Fate, who hath broken the wheels of my chariot! Oh, Pallas, thou hast undone me![214]

---

[213] An Athenian poet, who is said to have left one hundred and sixty tragedies behind him; he only once carried off the prize. Doubtless he had introduced gods or demi-gods bewailing themselves into one of his tragedies.

[214] This exclamation, "Oh! Pallas, thou hast undone me!" and the reply of Strepsiades are borrowed, says the scholiast, from a tragedy by Xenocles, the son of Carcinus. Alcmena is groaning over the death of her brother, Licymnius, who had been killed by Tlepolemus.

STREPSIADES. What ill has Tlepolemus done you?

AMYNIAS. Instead of jeering me, friend, make your son return me the money he has had of me; I am already unfortunate enough.

STREPSIADES. What money?

AMYNIAS. The money he borrowed of me.

STREPSIADES. You have indeed had misfortune, it seems to me.

AMYNIAS. Yes, by the gods! I have been thrown from a chariot.

STREPSIADES. Why then drivel as if you had fallen from an ass?[215]

AMYNIAS. Am I drivelling because I demand my money?

STREPSIADES. No, no, you cannot be in your right senses.

AMYNIAS. Why?

STREPSIADES. No doubt your poor wits have had a shake.

AMYNIAS. But by Hermes! I will sue you at law, if you do not pay me.

STREPSIADES. Just tell me; do you think it is always fresh water that Zeus lets fall every time it rains, or is it always the same water that the sun pumps over the earth?

AMYNIAS. I neither know, nor care.

STREPSIADES. And actually you would claim the right to demand your money, when you know not a syllable of these celestial phenomena?

AMYNIAS. If you are short, pay me the interest, at any rate.

STREPSIADES. What kind of animal is interest?

AMYNIAS. What? Does not the sum borrowed go on growing, growing every month, each day as the time slips by?

STREPSIADES. Well put. But do you believe there is more water in the sea now than there was formerly?

AMYNIAS. No, 'tis just the same quantity. It cannot increase.

STREPSIADES. Thus, poor fool, the sea, that receives the rivers, never grows, and yet you would have your money grow? Get you gone, away with you, quick! Ho! bring me the ox-goad!

AMYNIAS. Hither! you witnesses there!

STREPSIADES. Come, what are you waiting for? Will you not budge, old nag!

AMYNIAS. What an insult!

STREPSIADES. Unless you get a-trotting, I shall catch you and prick up your behind, you sorry packhorse! Ah! you start, do you? I was about to drive you pretty fast, I tell you—you and your wheels and your chariot!

CHORUS. Whither does the passion of evil lead! here is a perverse old man, who wants to cheat his creditors; but some mishap, which will speedily punish this rogue for his shameful schemings, cannot fail to overtake him from to-day. For a long time he has been burning to have his son know how to fight against all justice and right and to gain even the most iniquitous causes against his adversaries every one. I think this wish is going to be fulfilled. But mayhap, mayhap, he will soon wish his son were dumb rather!

STREPSIADES. Oh! oh! neighbours, kinsmen, fellow-citizens, help! help! to the rescue, I am being beaten! Oh! my head! oh! my jaw! Scoundrel! do you beat your own father!

PHIDIPPIDES. Yes, father, I do.

STREPSIADES. See! he admits he is beating me.

---

[215] A proverb, applied to foolish people.

PHIDIPPIDES. Undoubtedly I do.

STREPSIADES. You villain, you parricide, you gallows-bird!

PHIDIPPIDES. Go on, repeat your epithets, call me a thousand other names, an it please you. The more you curse, the greater my amusement!

STREPSIADES. Oh! you infamous cynic!

PHIDIPPIDES. How fragrant the perfume breathed forth in your words.

STREPSIADES. Do you beat your own father?

PHIDIPPIDES. Aye, by Zeus! and I am going to show you that I do right in beating you.

STREPSIADES. Oh, wretch! can it be right to beat a father?

PHIDIPPIDES. I will prove it to you, and you shall own yourself vanquished.

STREPSIADES. Own myself vanquished on a point like this?

PHIDIPPIDES. 'Tis the easiest thing in the world. Choose whichever of the two reasonings you like.

STREPSIADES. Of which reasonings?

PHIDIPPIDES. The Stronger and the Weaker.

STREPSIADES. Miserable fellow! Why, 'tis I who had you taught how to refute what is right, and now you would persuade me it is right a son should beat his father.

PHIDIPPIDES. I think I shall convince you so thoroughly that, when you have heard me, you will not have a word to say.

STREPSIADES. Well, I am curious to hear what you have to say.

CHORUS. Consider well, old man, how you can best triumph over him. His brazenness shows me that he thinks himself sure of his case; he has some argument which gives him nerve. Note the confidence in his look! But how did the fight begin? tell the Chorus; you cannot help doing that much.

STREPSIADES. I will tell you what was the start of the quarrel. At the end of the meal you wot of, I bade him take his lyre and sing me the air of Simonides, which tells of the fleece of the ram.[216] He replied bluntly, that it was stupid, while drinking, to play the lyre and sing, like a woman when she is grinding barley.

PHIDIPPIDES. Why, by rights I ought to have beaten and kicked you the very moment you told me to sing!

STREPSIADES. That is just how he spoke to me in the house, furthermore he added, that Simonides was a detestable poet. However, I mastered myself and for a while said nothing. Then I said to him, 'At least, take a myrtle branch and recite a passage from Aeschylus to me.'—'For my own part,' he at once replied, 'I look upon Aeschylus as the first of poets, for his verses roll superbly; 'tis nothing but incoherence, bombast and turgidness.' Yet still I smothered my wrath and said, 'Then recite one of the famous pieces from the modern poets.' Then he commenced a piece in which Euripides shows, oh! horror! a brother, who violates his own uterine sister.[217] Then I could no longer restrain myself, and attacked him with the most injurious abuse; naturally he retorted; hard words were hurled on both sides, and finally he sprang at me, broke my bones, bore me to earth, strangled and started killing me!

PHIDIPPIDES. I was right. What! not praise Euripides, the greatest of our poets!

STREPSIADES. He the greatest of our poets! Ah! if I but dared to speak! but the blows

---

[216] The ram of Phryxus, the golden fleece of which was hung up on a beech tree in a field dedicated to Ares in Colchis.

[217] The subject of Euripides' 'Aeolus.' Since among the Athenians it was lawful to marry a half-sister, if not born of the same mother, Strepsiades mentions here that it was his *uterine* sister, whom Macareus dishonoured, thus committing both rape and incest.

would rain upon me harder than ever.

PHIDIPPIDES. Undoubtedly, and rightly too.

STREPSIADES. Rightly! oh! what impudence! to me, who brought you up! when you could hardly lisp, I guessed what you wanted. If you said *broo, broo*, well, I brought you your milk; if you asked for *mam mam*, I gave you bread; and you had no sooner said, *caca*, than I took you outside and held you out. And just now, when you were strangling me, I shouted, I bellowed that I would let all go; and you, you scoundrel, had not the heart to take me outside, so that here, though almost choking, I was compelled to ease myself.

CHORUS. Young men, your hearts must be panting with impatience. What is Phidippides going to say? If, after such conduct, he proves he has done well, I would not give an obolus for the hide of old men. Come, you, who know how to brandish and hurl the keen shafts of the new science, find a way to convince us, give your language an appearance of truth.

PHIDIPPIDES. How pleasant it is to know these clever new inventions and to be able to defy the established laws! When I thought only about horses, I was not able to string three words together without a mistake, but now that the master has altered and improved me and that I live in this world of subtle thought, of reasoning and of meditation, I count on being able to prove satisfactorily that I have done well to thrash my father.

STREPSIADES. Mount your horse! By Zeus! I would rather defray the keep of a four-in-hand team than be battered with blows.

PHIDIPPIDES. I revert to what I was saying when you interrupted me. And first, answer me, did you beat me in my childhood?

STREPSIADES. Why, assuredly, for your good and in your own best interest.

PHIDIPPIDES. Tell me, is it not right, that in turn I should beat you for your good? since it is for a man's own best interest to be beaten. What! must your body be free of blows, and not mine? am I not free-born too? the children are to weep and the fathers go free?

STREPSIADES. But...

PHIDIPPIDES. You will tell me, that according to the law, 'tis the lot of children to be beaten. But I reply that the old men are children twice over and that it is far more fitting to chastise them than the young, for there is less excuse for their faults.

STREPSIADES. But the law nowhere admits that fathers should be treated thus.

PHIDIPPIDES. Was not the legislator who carried this law a man like you and me? In those days he got men to believe him; then why should not I too have the right to establish for the future a new law, allowing children to beat their fathers in turn? We make you a present of all the blows which were received before this law, and admit that you thrashed us with impunity. But look how the cocks and other animals fight with their fathers; and yet what difference is there betwixt them and ourselves, unless it be that they do not propose decrees?

STREPSIADES. But if you imitate the cocks in all things, why don't you scratch up the dunghill, why don't you sleep on a perch?

PHIDIPPIDES. That has no bearing on the case, good sir; Socrates would find no connection, I assure you.

STREPSIADES. Then do not beat at all, for otherwise you have only yourself to blame afterwards.

PHIDIPPIDES. What for?

STREPSIADES. I have the right to chastise you, and you to chastise your son, if you have one.

PHIDIPPIDES. And if I have not, I shall have cried in vain, and you will die laughing in my face.

STREPSIADES. What say you, all here present? It seems to me that he is right, and I am of opinion that they should be accorded their right. If we think wrongly, 'tis but just we should be beaten.

PHIDIPPIDES. Again, consider this other point.

STREPSIADES. 'Twill be the death of me.

PHIDIPPIDES. But you will certainly feel no more anger because of the blows I have given you.

STREPSIADES. Come, show me what profit I shall gain from it.

PHIDIPPIDES. I shall beat my mother just as I have you.

STREPSIADES. What do you say? what's that you say? Hah! this is far worse still.

PHIDIPPIDES. And what if I prove to you by our school reasoning, that one ought to beat one's mother?

STREPSIADES. Ah! if you do that, then you will only have to throw yourself along with Socrates and his reasoning, into the Barathrum.[218] Oh! Clouds! all our troubles emanate from you, from you, to whom I entrusted myself, body and soul.

CHORUS. No, you alone are the cause, because you have pursued the path of evil.

STREPSIADES. Why did you not say so then, instead of egging on a poor ignorant old man?

CHORUS. We always act thus, when we see a man conceive a passion for what is evil, we strike him with some terrible disgrace, so that he may learn to fear the gods.

STREPSIADES. Alas! oh Clouds! 'tis hard indeed, but 'tis just! I ought not to have cheated my creditors.... But come, my dear son, come with me to take vengeance on this wretched Chaerephon and on Socrates, who have deceived us both.

PHIDIPPIDES. I shall do nothing against our masters.

STREPSIADES. Oh! show some reverence for ancestral Zeus!

PHIDIPPIDES. Mark him and his ancestral Zeus! What a fool you are! Does any such being as Zeus exist?

STREPSIADES. Why, assuredly.

PHIDIPPIDES. No, a thousand times no! The ruler of the world is the Whirlwind, that has unseated Zeus.

STREPSIADES. He has not dethroned him. I believed it, because of this whirligig here. Unhappy wretch that I am! I have taken a piece of clay to be a god.

PHIDIPPIDES. Very well! Keep your stupid nonsense for your own consumption. [*Exit.*]

STREPSIADES. Oh! what madness! I had lost my reason when I threw over the gods through Socrates' seductive phrases. Oh! good Hermes, do not destroy me in your wrath. Forgive me; their babbling had driven me crazy. Be my councillor. Shall pursue them at law or shall I...? Order and I obey.—You are right, no law-suit; but up! let us burn down the home of those praters. Here, Xanthias, here! take a ladder, come forth and arm yourself with an axe; now mount upon the school, demolish the roof, if you love your master, and may the house fall in upon them, Ho! bring me a blazing torch! There is more than one of them, arch-impostors as they are, on whom I am determined to have vengeance.

---

[218] A cleft in the rocks at the back of the Acropolis at Athens, into which criminals were hurled.

A DISCIPLE. Oh! oh!

STREPSIADES. Come, torch, do your duty! Burst into full flame!

DISCIPLE. What are you up to?

STREPSIADES. What am I up to? Why, I am entering upon a subtle argument with the beams of the house.

SECOND DISCIPLE. Hullo! hullo! who is burning down our house?

STREPSIADES. The man whose cloak you have appropriated.

SECOND DISCIPLE. But we are dead men, dead men!

STREPSIADES. That is just exactly what I hope, unless my axe plays me false, or I fall and break my neck.

SOCRATES. Hi! you fellow on the roof, what are you doing up there?

STREPSIADES. I traverse the air and contemplate the sun.[219]

SOCRATES. Ah! ah! woe is upon me! I am suffocating!

CHAEREPHON. Ah! you insulted the gods! Ah! you studied the face of the moon! Chase them, strike and beat them down! Forward! they have richly deserved their fate—above all, by reason of their blasphemies.

CHORUS. So let the Chorus file off the stage. Its part is played.

---

[219] He repeats the words of Socrates at their first interview, in mockery.

# LYSISTRATA

## INTRODUCTION

The 'Lysistrata,' the third and concluding play of the War and Peace series, was not produced till ten years later than its predecessor, the 'Peace,' viz. in 411 B.C. It is now the twenty-first year of the War, and there seems as little prospect of peace as ever. A desperate state of things demands a desperate remedy, and the Poet proceeds to suggest a burlesque solution of the difficulty.

The women of Athens, led by Lysistrata and supported by female delegates from the other states of Hellas, determine to take matters into their own hands and force the men to stop the War. They meet in solemn conclave, and Lysistrata expounds her scheme, the rigorous application to husbands and lovers of a self-denying ordinance—"we must refrain from the male organ altogether." Every wife and mistress is to refuse all sexual favours whatsoever, till the men have come to terms of peace. In cases where the women *must* yield 'par force majeure,' then it is to be with an ill grace and in such a way as to afford the minimum of gratification to their partner; they are to lie passive and take no more part in the amorous game than they are absolutely obliged to. By these means Lysistrata assures them they will very soon gain their end. "If we sit indoors prettily dressed out in our best transparent silks and prettiest gewgaws, and with our 'mottes' all nicely depilated, their tools will stand up so stiff that they will be able to deny us nothing." Such is the burden of her advice.

After no little demur, this plan of campaign is adopted, and the assembled women take a solemn oath to observe the compact faithfully. Meantime as a precautionary measure they seize the Acropolis, where the State treasure is kept; the old men of the city assault the doors, but are repulsed by "the terrible regiment" of women. Before long the device of the bold Lysistrata proves entirely effective, Peace is concluded, and the play ends with the hilarious festivities of the Athenian and Spartan plenipotentiaries in celebration of the event.

This drama has a double Chorus—of women and of old men, and much excellent fooling is got out of the fight for possession of the citadel between the two hostile bands; while the broad jokes and decidedly suggestive situations arising out of the general idea of the plot outlined above may be "better imagined than described."

## DRAMATIS PERSONAE

LYSISTRATA
CALONICÉ
MYRRHINÉ
LAMPITO
STRATYLLIS
A MAGISTRATE
CINESIAS. A CHILD
HERALD OF THE LACEDAEMONIANS
ENVOYS OF THE LACEDAEMONIANS
POLYCHARIDES
MARKET LOUNGERS
A SERVANT
AN ATHENIAN CITIZEN
CHORUS OF OLD MEN
CHORUS OF WOMEN

SCENE: *In a public square at Athens; afterwards before the gates of the Acropolis, and finally within the precincts of the citadel.*

# LYSISTRATA

LYSISTRATA. [*alone.*] Ah! if only they had been invited to a Bacchic revelling, or a feast of Pan or Aphrodité or Genetyllis,[220] why! the streets would have been impassable for the thronging tambourines! Now there's never a woman here-ah! except my neighbour Calonicé, whom I see approaching yonder.... Good day, Calonicé.

CALONICÉ. Good day, Lysistrata; but pray, why this dark, forbidding face, my dear? Believe me, you don't look a bit pretty with those black lowering brows.

LYSISTRATA. Oh! Calonicé, my heart is on fire; I blush for our sex. Men *will* have it we are tricky and sly....

CALONICÉ. And they are quite right, upon my word!

LYSISTRATA. Yet, look you, when the women are summoned to meet for a matter of the last importance, they lie abed instead of coming.

CALONICÉ. Oh! they will come, my dear; but 'tis not easy, you know, for women to leave the house. One is busy pottering about her husband; another is getting the servant up; a third is putting her child asleep, or washing the brat or feeding it.

LYSISTRATA. But I tell you, the business that calls them here is far and away more urgent.

CALONICÉ. And why *do* you summon us, dear Lysistrata? What is it all about?

LYSISTRATA. About a big affair.[221]

CALONICÉ. And is it thick too?

LYSISTRATA. Yes indeed, both big and great.

CALONICÉ. And we are not all on the spot!

LYSISTRATA. Oh! if it were what you suppose, there would be never an absentee. No, no, it concerns a thing I have turned about and about this way and that of many sleepless nights.

CALONICÉ. It must be something mighty fine and subtle for you to have turned it about so!

LYSISTRATA. So fine, it means just this, Greece saved by the women!

CALONICÉ. By women! Why, its salvation hangs on a poor thread then!

LYSISTRATA. Our country's fortunes depend on us—it is with us to undo utterly the Peloponnesians.

CALONICÉ. That would be a noble deed truly!

LYSISTRATA. To exterminate the Boeotians to a man!

CALONICÉ. But surely you would spare the eels.[222]

---

[220] At Athens more than anywhere the festivals of Bacchus (Dionysus) were celebrated with the utmost pomp—and also with the utmost licence, not to say licentiousness.

Pan—the rustic god and king of the Satyrs; his feast was similarly an occasion of much coarse self-indulgence.

Aphrodité Colias—under this name the goddess was invoked by courtesans as patroness of sensual, physical love. She had a temple on the promontory of Colias, on the Attic coast—whence the surname.

The Genetyllides were minor deities, presiding over the act of generation, as the name indicates. Dogs were offered in sacrifice to them—presumably because of the lubricity of that animal.

At the festivals of Dionysus, Pan and Aphrodité women used to perform lascivious dances to the accompaniment of the beating of tambourines. Lysistrata implies that the women she had summoned to council cared really for nothing but wanton pleasures.

[221] An obscene *double entendre*; Calonicé understands, or pretends to understand, Lysistrata as meaning a long and thick "membrum virile"!

LYSISTRATA. For Athens' sake I will never threaten so fell a doom; trust me for that. However, if the Boeotian and Peloponnesian women join us, Greece is saved.

CALONICÉ. But how should women perform so wise and glorious an achievement, we women who dwell in the retirement of the household, clad in diaphanous garments of yellow silk and long flowing gowns, decked out with flowers and shod with dainty little slippers?

LYSISTRATA. Nay, but those are the very sheet-anchors of our salvation—those yellow tunics, those scents and slippers, those cosmetics and transparent robes.

CALONICÉ. How so, pray?

LYSISTRATA. There is not a man will wield a lance against another ...

CALONICÉ. Quick, I will get me a yellow tunic from the dyer's.

LYSISTRATA. ... or want a shield.

CALONICÉ. I'll run and put on a flowing gown.

LYSISTRATA. ... or draw a sword.

CALONICÉ. I'll haste and buy a pair of slippers this instant.

LYSISTRATA. Now tell me, would not the women have done best to come?

CALONICÉ. Why, they should have *flown* here!

LYSISTRATA. Ah! my dear, you'll see that like true Athenians, they will do everything too late.[223] ... Why, there's not a woman come from the shoreward parts, not one from Salamis.[224]

CALONICÉ. But I know for certain they embarked at daybreak.

LYSISTRATA. And the dames from Acharnae![225] why, I thought they would have been the very first to arrive.

CALONICÉ. Theagenes wife[226] at any rate is sure to come; she has actually been to consult Hecaté.... But look! here are some arrivals—and there are more behind. Ah! ha! now what countrywomen may they be?

LYSISTRATA. They are from Anagyra.[227]

CALONICÉ. Yes! upon my word, 'tis a levy *en masse* of all the female population of Anagyra!

MYRRHINÉ. Are we late, Lysistrata? Tell us, pray; what, not a word?

LYSISTRATA. I cannot say much for you, Myrrhiné! you have not bestirred yourself overmuch for an affair of such urgency.

MYRRHINÉ. I could not find my girdle in the dark. However, if the matter is so pressing, here we are; so speak.

LYSISTRATA. No, but let us wait a moment more, till the women of Boeotia arrive and those from the Peloponnese.

MYRRHINÉ. Yes, that is best.... Ah! here comes Lampito.

---

[222] The eels from Lake Copaïs in Boeotia were esteemed highly by epicures.

[223] This is the reproach Demosthenes constantly levelled against his Athenian fellow-countrymen—their failure to seize opportunity.

[224] An island of the Saronic Gulf, lying between Magara and Attica. It was separated by a narrow strait—scene of the naval battle of Salamis, in which the Athenians defeated Xerxes—only from the Attic coast, and was subject to Athens.

[225] A deme, or township, of Attica, lying five or six miles north of Athens. The Acharnians were throughout the most extreme partisans of the warlike party during the Peloponnesian struggle. See 'The Acharnians.'

[226] The precise reference is uncertain, and where the joke exactly comes in. The Scholiast says Theagenes was a rich, miserly and superstitious citizen, who never undertook any enterprise without first consulting an image of Hecaté, the distributor of honour and wealth according to popular belief; and his wife would naturally follow her husband's example.

[227] A deme of Attica, a small and insignificant community—a 'Little Pedlington' in fact.

LYSISTRATA. Good day, Lampito, dear friend from Lacedaemon. How well and handsome you look! what a rosy complexion! and how strong you seem; why, you could strangle a bull surely!

LAMPITO. Yes, indeed, I really think I could. 'Tis because I do gymnastics and practise the kick dance.[228]

LYSISTRATA. And what superb bosoms!

LAMPITO. La! you are feeling me as if I were a beast for sacrifice.

LYSISTRATA. And this young woman, what countrywoman is she?

LAMPITO. She is a noble lady from Boeotia.

LYSISTRATA. Ah! my pretty Boeotian friend, you are as blooming as a garden.

CALONICÉ. Yes, on my word! and the garden is so prettily weeded too![229]

LYSISTRATA. And who is this?

LAMPITO. 'Tis an honest woman, by my faith! she comes from Corinth.

LYSISTRATA. Oh! honest, no doubt then—as honesty goes at Corinth.[230]

LAMPITO. But who has called together this council of women, pray?

LYSISTRATA. I have.

LAMPITO. Well then, tell us what you want of us.

LYSISTRATA. With pleasure, my dear.

MYRRHINÉ. What is the most important business you wish to inform us about?

LYSISTRATA. I will tell you. But first answer me one question.

MYRRHINÉ. What is that?

LYSISTRATA. Don't you feel sad and sorry because the fathers of your children are far away from you with the army? For I'll undertake, there is not one of you whose husband is not abroad at this moment.

CALONICÉ. Mine has been the last five months in Thrace—looking after Eucrates.[231]

LYSISTRATA. 'Tis seven long months since mine left me for Pylos.[232]

LAMPITO. As for mine, if he ever does return from service, he's no sooner back than he takes down his shield again and flies back to the wars.

LYSISTRATA. And not so much as the shadow of a lover! Since the day the Milesians betrayed us, I have never once seen an eight-inch-long *godemiche* even, to be a leathern consolation to us poor widows.... Now tell me, if I have discovered a means of ending the war, will you all second me?

MYRRHINÉ. Yes verily, by all the goddesses, I swear I will, though I have to put my gown in pawn, and drink the money the same day.[233]

---

[228] In allusion to the gymnastic training which was *de rigueur* at Sparta for the women no less than the men, and in particular to the dance of the Lacedaemonian girls, in which the performer was expected to kick the fundament with the heels—always a standing joke among the Athenians against their rivals and enemies the Spartans.

[229] The allusion, of course, is to the 'garden of love,' the female parts, which it was the custom with the Greek women, as it is with the ladies of the harem in Turkey to this day, to depilate scrupulously, with the idea of making themselves more attractive to men.

[230] Corinth was notorious in the Ancient world for its prostitutes and general dissoluteness.

[231] An Athenian general strongly suspected of treachery; Aristophanes pretends his own soldiers have to see that he does not desert to the enemy.

[232] A town and fortress on the west coast of Messenia, south-east part of Peloponnese, at the northern extremity of the bay of Sphacteria—the scene by the by of the modern naval battle of Navarino—in Lacedaemonian territory; it had been seized by the Athenian fleet, and was still in their possession at the date, 412 B.C., of the representation of the 'Lysistrata,' though two years later, in the twenty-second year of the War, it was recovered by Sparta.

CALONICÉ. And so will I, though I must be split in two like a flat-fish, and have half myself removed.

LAMPITO. And I too; why, to secure Peace, I would climb to the top of Mount Taygetus.[234]

LYSISTRATA. Then I will out with it at last, my mighty secret! Oh! sister women, if we would compel our husbands to make peace, we must refrain....

MYRRHINÉ. Refrain from what? tell us, tell us!

LYSISTRATA. But will you do it?

MYRRHINÉ. We will, we will, though we should die of it.

LYSISTRATA. We must refrain from the male organ altogether.... Nay, why do you turn your backs on me? Where are you going? So, you bite your lips, and shake your heads, eh? Why these pale, sad looks? why these tears? Come, will you do it—yes or no? Do you hesitate?

MYRRHINÉ. No, I will not do it; let the War go on.

LYSISTRATA. And you, my pretty flat-fish, who declared just now they might split you in two?

CALONICÉ. Anything, anything but that! Bid me go through the fire, if you will; but to rob us of the sweetest thing in all the world, my dear, dear Lysistrata!

LYSISTRATA. And you?

MYRRHINÉ. Yes, I agree with the others; I too would sooner go through the fire.

LYSISTRATA. Oh, wanton, vicious sex! the poets have done well to make tragedies upon us; we are good for nothing then but love and lewdness![235] But you, my dear, you from hardy Sparta, if *you* join me, all may yet be well; help me, second me, I conjure you.

LAMPITO. 'Tis a hard thing, by the two goddesses[236] it is! for a woman to sleep alone without ever a standing weapon in her bed. But there, Peace must come first.

LYSISTRATA. Oh, my dear, my dearest, best friend, you are the only one deserving the name of woman!

CALONICÉ. But if—which the gods forbid—we do refrain altogether from what you say, should we get peace any sooner?

LYSISTRATA. Of course we should, by the goddesses twain! We need only sit indoors with painted cheeks, and meet our mates lightly clad in transparent gowns of Amorgos[237] silk, and with our "mottes" nicely plucked smooth; then their tools will stand like mad and they will be wild to lie with us. That will be the time to refuse, and they will hasten to make peace, I am convinced of that!

LAMPITO. Yes, just as Menelaus, when he saw Helen's naked bosom, threw away his sword, they say.

CALONICÉ. But, poor devils, suppose our husbands go away and leave us.

---

[233] The Athenian women, rightly or wrongly, had the reputation of being over fond of wine. Aristophanes, here and elsewhere, makes many jests on this weakness of theirs.

[234] The lofty range of hills overlooking Sparta from the west.

[235] In the original "we are nothing but Poseidon and a boat"; the allusion is to a play of Sophocles, now lost, but familiar to Aristophanes' audience, entitled 'Tyro,' in which the heroine, Tyro, appears with Poseidon, the sea-god, at the beginning of the tragedy, and at the close with the two boys she had had by him, whom she exposes in an open boat.

[236] "By the two goddesses,"—a woman's oath, which recurs constantly in this play; the two goddesses are always Demeter and Proserpine.

[237] One of the Cyclades, between Naxos and Cos, celebrated, like the latter, for its manufacture of fine, almost transparent silks, worn in Greece, and later at Rome, by women of loose character.

LYSISTRATA. Then, as Pherecrates says, we must "flay a skinned dog,"[238] that's all.

CALONICÉ. Bah! these proverbs are all idle talk.... But if our husbands drag us by main force into the bedchamber?

LYSISTRATA. Hold on to the door posts.

CALONICÉ. But if they beat us?

LYSISTRATA. Then yield to their wishes, but with a bad grace; there is no pleasure for them, when they do it by force. Besides, there are a thousand ways of tormenting them. Never fear, they'll soon tire of the game; there's no satisfaction for a man, unless the woman shares it.

CALONICÉ. Very well, if you *will* have it so, we agree.

LAMPITO. For ourselves, no doubt we shall persuade our husbands to conclude a fair and honest peace; but there is the Athenian populace, how are we to cure these folk of their warlike frenzy?

LYSISTRATA. Have no fear; we undertake to make our own people hear reason.

LAMPITO. Nay, impossible, so long as they have their trusty ships and the vast treasures stored in the temple of Athené.

LYSISTRATA. Ah! but we have seen to that; this very day the Acropolis will be in our hands. That is the task assigned to the older women; while we are here in council, they are going, under pretence of offering sacrifice, to seize the citadel.

LAMPITO. Well said indeed! so everything is going for the best.

LYSISTRATA. Come, quick, Lampito, and let us bind ourselves by an inviolable oath.

LAMPITO. Recite the terms; we will swear to them.

LYSISTRATA. With pleasure. Where is our Usheress?[239] Now, what are you staring at, pray? Lay this shield on the earth before us, its hollow upwards, and someone bring me the victim's inwards.

CALONICÉ. Lysistrata, say, what oath are we to swear?

LYSISTRATA. What oath? Why, in Aeschylus, they sacrifice a sheep, and swear over a buckler;[240] we will do the same.

CALONICÉ. No, Lysistrata, one cannot swear peace over a buckler, surely.

LYSISTRATA. What other oath do you prefer?

CALONICÉ. Let's take a white horse, and sacrifice it, and swear on its entrails.

LYSISTRATA. But where get a white horse from?

CALONICÉ. Well, what oath shall we take then?

LYSISTRATA. Listen to me. Let's set a great black bowl on the ground; let's sacrifice a skin of Thasian[241] wine into it, and take oath not to add one single drop of water.

LAMPITO. Ah! that's an oath pleases me more than I can say.

LYSISTRATA. Let them bring me a bowl and a skin of wine.

CALONICÉ. Ah! my dears, what a noble big bowl! what a delight 'twill be to empty it!

---

[238] The proverb, quoted by Pherecrates, is properly spoken of those who go out of their way to do a thing already done—"to kill a dead horse," but here apparently is twisted by Aristophanes into an allusion to the leathern 'godemiche' mentioned a little above; if the worst comes to the worst, we must use artificial means. Pherecrates was a comic playwright, a contemporary of Aristophanes.

[239] Literally "our Scythian woman." At Athens, policemen and ushers in the courts were generally Scythians; so the revolting women must have *their* Scythian "Usheress" too.

[240] In allusion to the oath which the seven allied champions before Thebes take upon a buckler, in Aeschylus' tragedy of 'The Seven against Thebes,' v. 42.

[241] A volcanic island in the northern part of the Aegaean, celebrated for its vineyards.

LYSISTRATA. Set the bowl down on the ground, and lay your hands on the victim.... Almighty goddess, Persuasion, and thou, bowl, boon comrade of joy and merriment, receive this our sacrifice, and be propitious to us poor women!

CALONICÉ. Oh! the fine red blood! how well it flows!

LAMPITO. And what a delicious savour, by the goddesses twain!

LYSISTRATA. Now, my dears, let me swear first, if you please.

CALONICÉ. No, by the goddess of love, let us decide that by lot.

LYSISTRATA. Come then, Lampito, and all of you, put your hands to the bowl; and do you, Calonicé, repeat in the name of all the solemn terms I am going to recite. Then you must all swear, and pledge yourselves by the same promises.—"*I will have naught to do whether with lover or husband....*"

CALONICÉ. *I will have naught to do whether with lover or husband....*

LYSISTRATA. *Albeit he come to me with stiff and standing tool....*

CALONICÉ. *Albeit he come to me with stiff and standing tool....* Oh! Lysistrata, I cannot bear it!

LYSISTRATA. *I will live at home in perfect chastity....*

CALONICÉ. *I will live at home in perfect chastity....*

LYSISTRATA. *Beautifully dressed and wearing a saffron-coloured gown....*

CALONICÉ. *Beautifully dressed and wearing a saffron-coloured gown....*

LYSISTRATA. *To the end I may inspire my husband with the most ardent longings.*

CALONICÉ. *To the end I may inspire my husband with the most ardent longings.*

LYSISTRATA. *Never will I give myself voluntarily....*

CALONICÉ. *Never will I give myself voluntarily....*

LYSISTRATA. *And if he has me by force....*

CALONICÉ. *And if he has me by force....*

LYSISTRATA. *I will be cold as ice, and never stir a limb....*

CALONICÉ. *I will be cold as ice, and never stir a limb....*

LYSISTRATA. *I will not lift my legs in air....*

CALONICÉ. *I will not lift my legs in air....*

LYSISTRATA. *Nor will I crouch with bottom upraised, like carven lions on a knife-handle.*

CALONICÉ. *Nor will I crouch with bottom upraised, like carven lions on a knife-handle.*

LYSISTRATA. *And if I keep my oath, may I be suffered to drink of this wine.*

CALONICÉ. *And if I keep my oath, may I be suffered to drink of this wine.*

LYSISTRATA. *But if I break it, let my bowl be filled with water.*

CALONICÉ. *But if I break it, let my bowl be filled with water.*

LYSISTRATA. Will ye all take this oath?

MYRRHINÉ. Yes, yes!

LYSISTRATA. Then lo! I immolate the victim. [*She drinks.*]

CALONICÉ. Enough, enough, my dear; now let us all drink in turn to cement our friendship.

LAMPITO. Hark! what do those cries mean?

LYSISTRATA. 'Tis what I was telling you; the women have just occupied the Acropolis. So now, Lampito, do you return to Sparta to organize the plot, while your comrades here remain as hostages. For ourselves, let us away to join the rest in the citadel, and let us push the bolts well home.

CALONICÉ. But don't you think the men will march up against us?

LYSISTRATA. I laugh at them. Neither threats nor flames shall force our doors; they shall open only on the conditions I have named.

CALONICÉ. Yes, yes, by the goddess of love! let us keep up our old-time repute for obstinacy and spite.

CHORUS OF OLD MEN.[242] Go easy, Draces, go easy; why, your shoulder is all chafed by these plaguey heavy olive stocks. But forward still, forward, man, as needs must. What unlooked-for things do happen, to be sure, in a long life! Ah! Strymodorus, who would ever have thought it? Here we have the women, who used, for our misfortune, to eat our bread and live in our houses, daring nowadays to lay hands on the holy image of the goddess, to seize the Acropolis and draw bars and bolts to keep any from entering! Come, Philurgus man, let's hurry thither; let's lay our faggots all about the citadel, and on the blazing pile burn with our hands these vile conspiratresses, one and all—and Lycon's wife, Lysistrata, first and foremost! Nay, by Demeter, never will I let 'em laugh at me, whiles I have a breath left in my body. Cleomenes himself,[243] the first who ever seized our citadel, had to quit it to his sore dishonour; spite his Lacedaemonian pride, he had to deliver me up his arms and slink off with a single garment to his back. My word! but he was filthy and ragged! and what an unkempt beard, to be sure! He had not had a bath for six long years! Oh! but that was a mighty siege! Our men were ranged seventeen deep before the gate, and never left their posts, even to sleep. These women, these enemies of Euripides and all the gods, shall I do nothing to hinder their inordinate insolence? else let them tear down my trophies of Marathon. But look ye, to finish our toilsome climb, we have only this last steep bit left to mount. Verily 'tis no easy job without beasts of burden, and how these logs do bruise my shoulder! Still let us on, and blow up our fire and see it does not go out just as we reach our destination. Phew! phew! [*blows the fire.*] Oh! dear! what a dreadful smoke! it bites my eyes like a mad dog. It is Lemnos[244] fire for sure, or it would never devour my eyelids like this. Come on, Laches, let's hurry, let's bring succour to the goddess; it's now or never! Phew! phew! [*blows the fire.*] Oh! dear! what a confounded smoke!—There now, there's our fire all bright and burning, thank the gods! Now, why not first put down our loads here, then take a vine-branch, light it at the brazier and hurl it at the gate by way of battering-ram? If they don't answer our summons by pulling back the bolts, then we set fire to the woodwork, and the smoke will choke 'em. Ye gods! what a smoke! Pfaugh! Is there never a Samos general will help me unload my burden?[245]—Ah! it shall not gall my shoulder any more. [*Tosses down his wood.*] Come, brazier, do your duty, make the embers flare, that I may kindle a brand; I want to be the first to hurl one. Aid me, heavenly Victory; let us punish for their insolent audacity the women who have seized our citadel, and may we raise a trophy of triumph for success!

---

[242] The old men are carrying faggots and fire to burn down the gates of the Acropolis, and supply comic material by their panting and wheezing as they climb the steep approaches to the fortress and puff and blow at their fires. Aristophanes gives them names, purely fancy ones—Draces, Strymodorus, Philurgus, Laches.

[243] Cleomenes, King of Sparta, had in the preceding century commanded a Lacedaemonian expedition against Athens. At the invitation of the Alcmaeonidae, enemies of the sons of Peisistratus, he seized the Acropolis, but after an obstinately contested siege was forced to capitulate and retire.

[244] Lemnos was proverbial with the Greeks for chronic misfortune and a succession of horrors and disasters. Can any good thing come out of *Lemnos*?

[245] That is, a friend of the Athenian people; Samos had just before the date of the play re-established the democracy and renewed the old alliance with Athens.

CHORUS OF WOMEN.[246] Oh! my dears, methinks I see fire and smoke; can it be a conflagration? Let us hurry all we can. Fly, fly, Nicodicé, ere Calycé and Crityllé perish in the fire, or are stifled in the smoke raised by these accursed old men and their pitiless laws. But, great gods, can it be I come too late? Rising at dawn, I had the utmost trouble to fill this vessel at the fountain. Oh! what a crowd there was, and what a din! What a rattling of water-pots! Servants and slave-girls pushed and thronged me! However, here I have it full at last; and I am running to carry the water to my fellow townswomen, whom our foes are plotting to burn alive. News has been brought us that a company of old, doddering greybeards, loaded with enormous faggots, as if they wanted to heat a furnace, have taken the field, vomiting dreadful threats, crying that they must reduce to ashes these horrible women. Suffer them not, oh! goddess, but, of thy grace, may I see Athens and Greece cured of their warlike folly. 'Tis to this end, oh! thou guardian deity of our city, goddess of the golden crest, that they have seized thy sanctuary. Be their friend and ally, Athené, and if any man hurl against them lighted firebrands, aid us to carry water to extinguish them.

STRATYLLIS. Let me be, I say. Oh! oh! [*She calls for help.*]

CHORUS OF WOMEN. What is this I see, ye wretched old men? Honest and pious folk ye cannot be who act so vilely.

CHORUS OF OLD MEN. Ah, ha! here's something new! a swarm of women stand posted outside to defend the gates!

CHORUS OF WOMEN. Ah! ah! we frighten you, do we; we seem a mighty host, yet you do not see the ten-thousandth part of our sex.

CHORUS OF OLD MEN. Ho, Phaedrias! shall we stop their cackle? Suppose one of us were to break a stick across their backs, eh?

CHORUS OF WOMEN. Let us set down our water-pots on the ground, to be out of the way, if they should dare to offer us violence.

CHORUS OF OLD MEN. Let someone knock out two or three teeth for them, as they did to Bupalus;[247] they won't talk so loud then.

CHORUS OF WOMEN. Come on then; I wait you with unflinching foot, and I will snap off your testicles like a bitch.

CHORUS OF OLD MEN. Silence! ere my stick has cut short your days.

CHORUS OF WOMEN. Now, just you dare to touch Stratyllis with the tip of your finger!

CHORUS OF OLD MEN. And if I batter you to pieces with my fists, what will you do?

CHORUS OF WOMEN. I will tear out your lungs and entrails with my teeth.

CHORUS OF OLD MEN. Oh! what a clever poet is Euripides! how well he says that woman is the most shameless of animals.

CHORUS OF WOMEN. Let's pick up our water-jars again, Rhodippé.

CHORUS OF OLD MEN. Ah! accursed harlot, what do you mean to do here with your water?

---

[246] A second Chorus enters—of women who are hurrying up with water to extinguish the fire just started by the Chorus of old men. Nicodicé, Calycé, Crityllé, Rhodippé, are fancy names the poet gives to different members of the band. Another, Stratyllis, has been stopped by the old men on her way to rejoin her companions.

[247] Bupalus was a celebrated contemporary sculptor, a native of Clazomenae. The satiric poet Hipponax, who was extremely ugly, having been portrayed by Bupalus as even more unsightly-looking than the reality, composed against the artist so scurrilous an invective that the latter hung himself in despair. Apparently Aristophanes alludes here to a verse in which Hipponax threatened to beat Bupalus.

CHORUS OF WOMEN. And you, old death-in-life, with your fire? Is it to cremate yourself?

CHORUS OF OLD MEN. I am going to build you a pyre to roast your female friends upon.

CHORUS OF WOMEN. And I,—I am going to put out your fire.

CHORUS OF OLD MEN. You put out my fire—you!

CHORUS OF WOMEN. Yes, you shall soon see.

CHORUS OF OLD MEN. I don't know what prevents me from roasting you with this torch.

CHORUS OF WOMEN. I am getting you a bath ready to clean off the filth.

CHORUS OF OLD MEN. A bath for me, you dirty slut, you!

CHORUS OF WOMEN. Yes, indeed, a nuptial bath—he, he!

CHORUS OF OLD MEN. Do you hear that? What insolence!

CHORUS OF WOMEN. I am a free woman, I tell you.

CHORUS OF OLD MEN. I will make you hold your tongue, never fear!

CHORUS OF WOMEN. Ah, ha! you shall never sit more amongst the Heliasts.[248]

CHORUS OF OLD MEN. Burn off her hair for her!

CHORUS OF WOMEN. Water, do your office! [*The women pitch the water in their water-pots over the old men.*]

CHORUS OF OLD MEN. Oh, dear! oh, dear! oh, dear!

CHORUS OF WOMEN. Was it hot?

CHORUS OF OLD MEN. Hot, great gods! Enough, enough!

CHORUS OF WOMEN. I'm watering you, to make you bloom afresh.

CHORUS OF OLD MEN. Alas! I am too dry! Ah, me! how I am trembling with cold!

MAGISTRATE. These women, have they made din enough, I wonder, with their tambourines? bewept Adonis enough upon their terraces?[249] I was listening to the speeches last assembly day,[250] and Demostratus,[251] whom heaven confound! was saying we must all go over to Sicily—and lo! his wife was dancing round repeating: Alas! alas! Adonis, woe is me for Adonis!

    Demostratus was saying we must levy hoplites at Zacynthus[252]—and lo! his wife, more than half drunk, was screaming on the house-roof: "Weep, weep for Adonis!"—while that infamous *Mad Ox*[253] was bellowing away on his side.—Do ye not blush, ye women, for your wild and uproarious doings?

---

[248] The Heliasts at Athens were the body of citizens chosen by lot to act as jurymen (or, more strictly speaking, as judges and jurymen, the Dicast, or so-called Judge, being merely President of the Court, the majority of the Heliasts pronouncing sentence) in the Heliaia, or High Court, where all offences liable to public prosecution were tried. They were 6000 in number, divided into ten panels of 500 each, a thousand being held in reserve to supply occasional vacancies. Each Heliast was paid three obols for each day's attendance in court.

[249] Women only celebrated the festivals of Adonis. These rites were not performed in public, but on the terraces and flat roofs of the houses.

[250] The Assembly, or Ecclesia, was the General Parliament of the Athenian people, in which every adult citizen had a vote. It met on the Pnyx hill, where the assembled Ecclesiasts were addressed from the Bema, or speaking-block.

[251] An orator and statesman who had first proposed the disastrous Sicilian Expedition, of 415-413 B.C. This was on the first day of the festival of Adonis—ever afterwards regarded by the Athenians as a day of ill omen.

[252] An island in the Ionian Sea, on the west of Greece, near Cephalenia, and an ally of Athens during the Peloponnesian War.

[253] Cholozyges, a nickname for Demostratus.

CHORUS OF OLD MEN. But you don't know all their effrontery yet! They abused and insulted us; then soused us with the water in their water-pots, and have set us wringing out our clothes, for all the world as if we had bepissed ourselves.

MAGISTRATE. And 'tis well done too, by Poseidon! We men must share the blame of their ill conduct; it is we who teach them to love riot and dissoluteness and sow the seeds of wickedness in their hearts. You see a husband go into a shop: "Look you, jeweller," says he, "you remember the necklace you made for my wife. Well, t'other evening, when she was dancing, the catch came open. Now, I am bound to start for Salamis; will you make it convenient to go up to-night to make her fastening secure?" Another will go to a cobbler, a great, strong fellow, with a great, long tool, and tell him: "The strap of one of my wife's sandals presses her little toe, which is extremely sensitive; come in about midday to supple the thing and stretch it." Now see the results. Take my own case—as a Magistrate I have enlisted rowers; I want money to pay 'em, and lo! the women clap to the door in my face.[254] But why do we stand here with arms crossed? Bring me a crowbar; I'll chastise their insolence!— Ho! there, my fine fellow! [addressing one of his attendant officers] what are you gaping at the crows about? looking for a tavern, I suppose, eh? Come, crowbars here, and force open the gates. I will put a hand to the work myself.

LYSISTRATA. No need to force the gates; I am coming out—here I am. And why bolts and bars? What we want here is not bolts and bars and locks, but common sense.

MAGISTRATE. Really, my fine lady! Where is my officer? I want him to tie that woman's hands behind her back.

LYSISTRATA. By Artemis, the virgin goddess! if he touches me with the tip of his finger, officer of the public peace though he be, let him look out for himself!

MAGISTRATE. [to the officer.] How now, are you afraid? Seize her, I tell you, round the body. Two of you at her, and have done with it!

FIRST WOMAN. By Pandrosos! if you lay a hand on her, I'll trample you underfoot till you shit your guts!

MAGISTRATE. Oh, there! my guts! Where is my other officer? Bind that minx first, who speaks so prettily!

SECOND WOMAN. By Phoebé, if you touch her with one finger, you'd better call quick for a surgeon!

MAGISTRATE. What do you mean? Officer, where are you got to? Lay hold of her. Oh! but I'm going to stop your foolishness for you all!

THIRD WOMAN. By the Tauric Artemis, if you go near her, I'll pull out your hair, scream as you like.

MAGISTRATE. Ah! miserable man that I am! My own officers desert me. What ho! are we to let ourselves be bested by a mob of women? Ho! Scythians mine, close up your ranks, and forward!

LYSISTRATA. By the holy goddesses! you'll have to make acquaintance with four companies of women, ready for the fray and well armed to boot.

MAGISTRATE. Forward, Scythians, and bind them!

LYSISTRATA. Forward, my gallant companions; march forth, ye vendors of grain and eggs, garlic and vegetables, keepers of taverns and bakeries, wrench and strike and tear; come, a torrent of invective and insult! [They beat the officers.] Enough, enough! now retire, never rob the vanquished!

---

[254] The State treasure was kept in the Acropolis, which the women had seized.

MAGISTRATE. Here's a fine exploit for my officers!

LYSISTRATA. Ah, ha! so you thought you had only to do with a set of slave-women! you did not know the ardour that fills the bosom of free-born dames.

MAGISTRATE. Ardour! yes, by Apollo, ardour enough—especially for the wine-cup!

CHORUS OF OLD MEN. Sir, sir! what use of words? they are of no avail with wild beasts of this sort. Don't you know how they have just washed us down—and with no very fragrant soap!

CHORUS OF WOMEN. What would you have? You should never have laid rash hands on us. If you start afresh, I'll knock your eyes out. My delight is to stay at home as coy as a young maid, without hurting anybody or moving any more than a milestone; but 'ware the wasps, if you go stirring up the wasps' nest!

CHORUS OF OLD MEN. Ah! great gods! how get the better of these ferocious creatures? 'tis past all bearing! But come, let us try to find out the reason of the dreadful scourge. With what end in view have they seized the citadel of Cranaus,[255] the sacred shrine that is raised upon the inaccessible rock of the Acropolis? Question them; be cautious and not too credulous. 'Twould be culpable negligence not to pierce the mystery, if we may.

MAGISTRATE. [*addressing the women.*] I would ask you first why ye have barred our gates.

LYSISTRATA. To seize the treasury; no more money, no more war.

MAGISTRATE. Then money is the cause of the War?

LYSISTRATA. And of all our troubles. 'Twas to find occasion to steal that Pisander[256] and all the other agitators were for ever raising revolutions. Well and good! but they'll never get another drachma here.

MAGISTRATE. What do you propose to do then, pray?

LYSISTRATA. You ask me that! Why, we propose to administer the treasury ourselves.

MAGISTRATE. *You* do?

LYSISTRATA. What is there in that to surprise you? Do we not administer the budget of household expenses?

MAGISTRATE. But that is not the same thing.

LYSISTRATA How so—not the same thing?

MAGISTRATE. It is the treasury supplies the expenses of the War.

LYSISTRATA. That's our first principle—no War!

MAGISTRATE. What! and the safety of the city?

LYSISTRATA. We will provide for that.

MAGISTRATE You?

LYSISTRATA Yes, just we.

MAGISTRATE. What a sorry business!

LYSISTRATA. Yes, we're going to save you, whether you will or no.

MAGISTRATE. Oh! the impudence of the creatures!

LYSISTRATA. You seem annoyed! but there, you've got to come to it.

MAGISTRATE. But 'tis the very height of iniquity!

LYSISTRATA. We're going to save you, my man.

MAGISTRATE. But if I don't want to be saved?

LYSISTRATA. Why, all the more reason!

---

[255] The second (mythical) king of Athens, successor of Cecrops.

[256] The leader of the Revolution which resulted in the temporary overthrow of the Democracy at Athens (413, 412 B.C.), and the establishment of the Oligarchy of the Four Hundred.

MAGISTRATE. But what a notion, to concern yourselves with questions of Peace and War!

LYSISTRATA. We will explain our idea.

MAGISTRATE. Out with it then; quick, or … [*threatening her.*]

LYSISTRATA. Listen, and never a movement, please!

MAGISTRATE. Oh! it is too much for me! I cannot keep my temper!

A WOMAN. Then look out for yourself; you have more to fear than we have.

MAGISTRATE. Stop your croaking, old crow, you! [*To Lysistrata.*] Now you, say your say.

LYSISTRATA. Willingly. All the long time the War has lasted, we have endured in modest silence all you men did; we never allowed ourselves to open our lips. We were far from satisfied, for we knew how things were going; often in our homes we would hear you discussing, upside down and inside out, some important turn of affairs. Then with sad hearts, but smiling lips, we would ask you: Well, in to-day's Assembly did they vote Peace?—But, "Mind your own business!" the husband would growl, "Hold your tongue, do!" And I would say no more.

A WOMAN. I would not have held my tongue though, not I!

MAGISTRATE. You would have been reduced to silence by blows then.

LYSISTRATA. Well, for my part, I would say no more. But presently I would come to know you had arrived at some fresh decision more fatally foolish than ever. "Ah! my dear man," I would say, "what madness next!" But he would only look at me askance and say: "Just weave your web, do; else your cheeks will smart for hours. War is men's business!"

MAGISTRATE. Bravo! well said indeed!

LYSISTRATA. How now, wretched man? not to let us contend against your follies, was bad enough! But presently we heard you asking out loud in the open street: "Is there never a man left in Athens?" and, "No, not one, not one," you were assured in reply. Then, then we made up our minds without more delay to make common cause to save Greece. Open your ears to our wise counsels and hold your tongues, and we may yet put things on a better footing.

MAGISTRATE. *You* put things indeed! Oh! 'tis too much! The insolence of the creatures! Silence, I say.

LYSISTRATA. Silence yourself!

MAGISTRATE. May I die a thousand deaths ere I obey one who wears a veil!

LYSISTRATA. If that's all that troubles you, here, take my veil, wrap it round your head, and hold your tongue. Then take this basket; put on a girdle, card wool, munch beans. The War shall be women's business.

CHORUS OF WOMEN. Lay aside your water-pots, we will guard them, we will help our friends and companions. For myself, I will never weary of the dance; my knees will never grow stiff with fatigue. I will brave everything with my dear allies, on whom Nature has lavished virtue, grace, boldness, cleverness, and whose wisely directed energy is going to save the State. Oh! my good, gallant Lysistrata, and all my friends, be ever like a bundle of nettles; never let your anger slacken; the winds of fortune blow our way.

LYSISTRATA. May gentle Love and the sweet Cyprian Queen shower seductive charms on our bosoms and all our person. If only we may stir so amorous a lust among the men that their tools stand stiff as sticks, we shall indeed deserve the name of peace-makers among the Greeks.

MAGISTRATE. How will that be, pray?

LYSISTRATA. To begin with, we shall not see you any more running like mad fellows to the Market holding lance in fist.

A WOMAN. That will be something gained, anyway, by the Paphian goddess, it will!

LYSISTRATA. Now we see 'em, mixed up with saucepans and kitchen stuff, armed to the teeth, looking like wild Corybantes![257]

MAGISTRATE. Why, of course; that's how brave men should do.

LYSISTRATA. Oh! but what a funny sight, to behold a man wearing a Gorgon's-head buckler coming along to buy fish!

A WOMAN. 'Tother day in the Market I saw a phylarch[258] with flowing ringlets; he was a-horseback, and was pouring into his helmet the broth he had just bought at an old dame's stall. There was a Thracian warrior too, who was brandishing his lance like Tereus in the play;[259] he had scared a good woman selling figs into a perfect panic, and was gobbling up all her ripest fruit.

MAGISTRATE. And how, pray, would you propose to restore peace and order in all the countries of Greece?

LYSISTRATA. 'Tis the easiest thing in the world!

MAGISTRATE. Come, tell us how; I am curious to know.

LYSISTRATA. When we are winding thread, and it is tangled, we pass the spool across and through the skein, now this way, now that way; even so, to finish off the War, we shall send embassies hither and thither and everywhere, to disentangle matters.

MAGISTRATE. And 'tis with your yarn, and your skeins, and your spools, you think to appease so many bitter enmities, you silly women?

LYSISTRATA. If only you had common sense, you would always do in politics the same as we do with our yarn.

MAGISTRATE. Come, how is that, eh?

LYSISTRATA. First we wash the yarn to separate the grease and filth; do the same with all bad citizens, sort them out and drive them forth with rods—'tis the refuse of the city. Then for all such as come crowding up in search of employments and offices, we must card them thoroughly; then, to bring them all to the same standard, pitch them pell-mell into the same basket, resident aliens or no, allies, debtors to the State, all mixed up together. Then as for our Colonies, you must think of them as so many isolated hanks; find the ends of the separate threads, draw them to a centre here, wind them into one, make one great hank of the lot, out of which the Public can weave itself a good, stout tunic.

MAGISTRATE. Is it not a sin and a shame to see them carding and winding the State, these women who have neither art nor part in the burdens of the War?

LYSISTRATA. What! wretched man! why, 'tis a far heavier burden to us than to you. In the first place, we bear sons who go off to fight far away from Athens.

MAGISTRATE. Enough said! do not recall sad and sorry memories![260]

---

[257] Priests of Cybelé, who indulged in wild, frenzied dances, to the accompaniment of the clashing of cymbals, in their celebrations in honour of the goddess.

[258] Captain of a cavalry division; they were chosen from amongst the *Hippeis*, or 'Knights' at Athens.

[259] In allusion to a play of Euripides, now lost, with this title. Tereus was son of Ares and king of the Thracians in Daulis.

[260] An allusion to the disastrous Sicilian Expedition (415-413 B.C.), in which many thousands of Athenian citizens perished.

LYSISTRATA. Then secondly, instead of enjoying the pleasures of love and making the best of our youth and beauty, we are left to languish far from our husbands, who are all with the army. But say no more of ourselves; what afflicts me is to see our girls growing old in lonely grief.

MAGISTRATE. Don't the men grow old too?

LYSISTRATA. That is not the same thing. When the soldier returns from the wars, even though he has white hair, he very soon finds a young wife. But a woman has only one summer; if she does not make hay while the sun shines, no one will afterwards have anything to say to her, and she spends her days consulting oracles, that never send her a husband.

MAGISTRATE. But the old man who can still erect his organ ...

LYSISTRATA. But you, why don't you get done with it and die? You are rich; go buy yourself a bier, and I will knead you a honey-cake for Cerberus. Here, take this garland. [*Drenching him with water.*]

FIRST WOMAN. And this one too. [*Drenching him with water.*]

SECOND WOMAN. And these fillets. [*Drenching him with water.*]

LYSISTRATA. What do you lack more? Step aboard the boat; Charon is waiting for you, you're keeping him from pushing off.

MAGISTRATE. To treat me so scurvily! What an insult! I will go show myself to my fellow-magistrates just as I am.

LYSISTRATA. What! are you blaming us for not having exposed you according to custom?[261] Nay, console yourself; we will not fail to offer up the third-day sacrifice for you, first thing in the morning.[262]

CHORUS OF OLD MEN. Awake, friends of freedom; let us hold ourselves aye ready to act. I suspect a mighty peril; I foresee another Tyranny like Hippias'.[263] I am sore afraid the Laconians assembled here with Cleisthenes have, by a stratagem of war, stirred up these women, enemies of the gods, to seize upon our treasury and the funds whereby I lived.[264] Is it not a sin and a shame for them to interfere in advising the citizens, to prate of shields and lances, and to ally themselves with Laconians, fellows I trust no more than I would so many famished wolves? The whole thing, my friends, is nothing else but an attempt to re-establish Tyranny. But I will never submit; I will be on my guard for the future; I will always carry a blade hidden under myrtle boughs; I will post myself in the Public Square under arms, shoulder to shoulder with Aristogiton;[265] and now, to make a start, I must just break a few of that cursed old jade's teeth yonder.

CHORUS OF WOMEN. Nay, never play the brave man, else when you go back home, your own mother won't know you. But, dear friends and allies, first let us lay our burdens down; then, citizens all, hear what I have to say. I have useful counsel to give our city, which deserves it well at my hands for the brilliant distinctions it has

---

[261] The dead were laid out at Athens before the house door.

[262] An offering made to the Manes of the deceased on the third day after the funeral.

[263] Hippias and Hipparchus, the two sons of Pisistratus, known as the Pisistratidae, became Tyrants of Athens upon their father's death in 527 B.C. In 514 the latter was assassinated by the conspirators, Harmodius and Aristogiton, who took the opportunity of the Panathenaic festival and concealed their daggers in myrtle wreaths. They were put to death, but four years later the surviving Tyrant Hippias was expelled, and the young and noble martyrs to liberty were ever after held in the highest honour by their fellow-citizens. Their statues stood in the Agora or Public Market-Square.

[264] That is, the three obols paid for attendance as a Heliast at the High Court.

[265] See above, under note 263.

lavished on my girlhood. At seven years of age, I was bearer of the sacred vessels; at ten, I pounded barley for the altar of Athené; next, clad in a robe of yellow silk, I was *little bear* to Artemis at the Brauronia;[266] presently, grown a tall, handsome maiden, they put a necklace of dried figs about my neck, and I was Basket-Bearer.[267] So surely I am bound to give my best advice to Athens. What matters that I was born a woman, if I can cure your misfortunes? I pay my share of tolls and taxes, by giving men to the State. But you, you miserable greybeards, you contribute nothing to the public charges; on the contrary, you have wasted the treasure of our forefathers, as it was called, the treasure amassed in the days of the Persian Wars.[268] You pay nothing at all in return; and into the bargain you endanger our lives and liberties by your mistakes. Have you one word to say for yourselves? ... Ah! don't irritate me, you there, or I'll lay my slipper across your jaws; and it's pretty heavy.

CHORUS OF OLD MEN. Outrage upon outrage! things are going from bad to worse. Let us punish the minxes, every one of us that has a man's appendages to boast of. Come, off with our tunics, for a man must savour of manhood; come, my friends, let us strip naked from head to foot. Courage, I say, we who in our day garrisoned Lipsydrion;[269] let us be young again, and shake off eld. If we give them the least hold over us, 'tis all up! their audacity will know no bounds! We shall see them building ships, and fighting sea-fights, like Artemisia;[270] nay, if they want to mount and ride as cavalry, we had best cashier the knights, for indeed women excel in riding, and have a fine, firm seat for the gallop.[271] Just think of all those squadrons of Amazons Micon has painted for us engaged in hand-to-hand combat with men.[272] Come then, we must e'en fit collars to all these willing necks.

CHORUS OF WOMEN. By the blessed goddesses, if you anger me, I will let loose the beast of my evil passions, and a very hailstorm of blows will set you yelling for help. Come, dames, off tunics, and quick's the word; women must scent the savour of women in the throes of passion.... Now just you dare to measure strength with me, old greybeard, and I warrant you you'll never eat garlic or black beans more. No, not a word! my anger is at boiling point, and I'll do with you what the beetle did with the

---

[266] The origin of the name was this: in ancient days a tame bear consecrated to Artemis, the huntress goddess, it seems, devoured a young girl, whose brothers killed the offender. Artemis was angered and sent a terrible pestilence upon the city, which only ceased when, by direction of the oracle, a company of maidens was dedicated to the deity, to act the part of she-bears in the festivities held annually in her honour at the *Brauronia*, her festival so named from the deme of Brauron in Attica.

[267] The Basket-Bearers, Canephoroi, at Athens were the maidens who, clad in flowing robes, carried in baskets on their heads the sacred implements and paraphernalia in procession at the celebrations in honour of Demeter, Dionysus and Athené.

[268] A treasure formed by voluntary contributions at the time of the Persian Wars; by Aristophanes' day it had all been dissipated, through the influence of successive demagogues, in distributions and gifts to the public under various pretexts.

[269] A town and fortress of Southern Attica, in the neighbourhood of Marathon, occupied by the Alcmaeonidae—the noble family or clan at Athens banished from the city in 595 B.C., restored 560, but again expelled by Pisistratus—in the course of their contest with that Tyrant. Returning to Athens on the death of Hippias (510 B.C.), they united with the democracy, and the then head of the family, Cleisthenes, gave a new constitution to the city.

[270] Queen of Halicarnassus, in Caria; an ally of the Persian King Xerxes in his invasion of Greece; she fought gallantly at the battle of Salamis.

[271] A *double entendre*—with allusion to the posture in sexual intercourse known among the Greeks as [Greek: hippos], in Latin 'equus,' the horse, where the woman mounts the man in reversal of the ordinary position.

[272] Micon, a famous Athenian painter, decorated the walls of the Poecilé Stoa, or Painted Porch, at Athens with a series of frescoes representing the battles of the Amazons with Theseus and the Athenians.

eagle's eggs.[273] I laugh at your threats, so long as I have on my side Lampito here, and the noble Theban, my dear Ismenia.... Pass decree on decree, you can do us no hurt, you wretch abhorred of all your fellows. Why, only yesterday, on occasion of the feast of Hecaté, I asked my neighbours of Boeotia for one of their daughters for whom my girls have a lively liking—a fine, fat eel to wit; and if they did not refuse, all along of your silly decrees! We shall never cease to suffer the like, till someone gives you a neat trip-up and breaks your neck for you!

[*Several days are supposed to have elapsed.*]

CHORUS OF WOMEN. [*addressing Lysistrata.*] You, Lysistrata, you who are leader of our glorious enterprise, why do I see you coming towards me with so gloomy an air?

LYSISTRATA. 'Tis the behaviour of these naughty women, 'tis the female heart and female weakness so discourages me.

CHORUS OF WOMEN. Tell us, tell us, what is it?

LYSISTRATA. I only tell the simple truth.

CHORUS OF WOMEN. What has happened so disconcerting; come, tell your friends.

LYSISTRATA. Oh! the thing is so hard to tell—yet so impossible to conceal.

CHORUS OF WOMEN. Nay, never seek to hide any ill that has befallen our cause.

LYSISTRATA. To blurt it out in a word—we are in heat!

CHORUS OF WOMEN. Oh! Zeus, oh! Zeus!

LYSISTRATA. What use calling upon Zeus? The thing is even as I say. I cannot stop them any longer from lusting after the men. They are all for deserting. The first I caught was slipping out by the postern gate near the cave of Pan; another was letting herself down by a rope and pulley; a third was busy preparing her escape; while a fourth, perched on a bird's back, was just taking wing for Orsilochus' house,[274] when I seized her by the hair. One and all, they are inventing excuses to be off home. Look! there goes one, trying to get out! Halloa there! whither away so fast?

FIRST WOMAN. I want to go home; I have some Miletus wool in the house, which is getting all eaten up by the worms.

LYSISTRATA. Bah! you and your worms! go back, I say!

FIRST WOMAN. I will return immediately, I swear I will by the two goddesses! I only have just to spread it out on the bed.

LYSISTRATA. You shall not do anything of the kind! I say, you shall not go.

FIRST WOMAN. Must I leave my wool to spoil then?

LYSISTRATA. Yes, if need be.

SECOND WOMAN. Unhappy woman that I am! Alas for my flax! I've left it at home unstript!

LYSISTRATA. So, here's another trying to escape to go home and strip her flax forsooth!

SECOND WOMAN. Oh! I swear by the goddess of light, the instant I have put it in condition I will come straight back.

LYSISTRATA. You shall do nothing of the kind! If once you began, others would want to follow suit.

---

[273] To avenge itself on the eagle, the beetle threw the former's eggs out of the nest and broke them. See the Fables of Aesop.

[274] Keeper of a house of ill fame apparently.

THIRD WOMAN. Oh! goddess divine, Ilithyia, patroness of women in labour, stay, stay the birth, till I have reached a spot less hallowed than Athené's Mount!

LYSISTRATA. What mean you by these silly tales?

THIRD WOMAN. I am going to have a child—now, this minute.

LYSISTRATA. But you were not pregnant yesterday!

THIRD WOMAN. Well, I am to-day. Oh! let me go in search of the midwife, Lysistrata, quick, quick!

LYSISTRATA. What is this fable you are telling me? Ah! what have you got there so hard?

THIRD WOMAN. A male child.

LYSISTRATA. No, no, by Aphrodité! nothing of the sort! Why, it feels like something hollow—a pot or a kettle. Oh! you baggage, if you have not got the sacred helmet of Pallas—and you said you were with child!

THIRD WOMAN. And so I am, by Zeus, I am!

LYSISTRATA. Then why this helmet, pray?

THIRD WOMAN. For fear my pains should seize me in the Acropolis; I mean to lay my eggs in this helmet, as the doves do.

LYSISTRATA. Excuses and pretences every word! the thing's as clear as daylight. Anyway, you must stay here now till the fifth day, your day of purification.

THIRD WOMAN. I cannot sleep any more in the Acropolis, now I have seen the snake that guards the Temple.

FOURTH WOMAN. Ah! and those confounded owls with their dismal hooting! I cannot get a wink of rest, and I'm just dying of fatigue.

LYSISTRATA. You wicked women, have done with your falsehoods! You want your husbands, that's plain enough. But don't you think they want you just as badly? They are spending dreadful nights, oh! I know that well enough. But hold out, my dears, hold out! A little more patience, and the victory will be ours. An Oracle promises us success, if only we remain united. Shall I repeat the words?

FIRST WOMAN. Yes, tell us what the Oracle declares.

LYSISTRATA. Silence then! Now—"Whenas the swallows, fleeing before the hoopoes, shall have all flocked together in one place, and shall refrain them from all amorous commerce, then will be the end of all the ills of life; yea, and Zeus, which doth thunder in the skies, shall set above what was erst below...."

CHORUS OF WOMEN. What! shall the men be underneath?

LYSISTRATA. "But if dissension do arise among the swallows, and they take wing from the holy Temple, 'twill be said there is never a more wanton bird in all the world."

CHORUS OF WOMEN. Ye gods! the prophecy is clear. Nay, never let us be cast down by calamity! let us be brave to bear, and go back to our posts. 'Twere shameful indeed not to trust the promises of the Oracle.

CHORUS OF OLD MEN. I want to tell you a fable they used to relate to me when I was a little boy. This is it: Once upon a time there was a young man called Melanion, who hated the thought of marriage so sorely that he fled away to the wilds. So he dwelt in the mountains, wove himself nets, kept a dog and caught hares. He never, never came back, he had such a horror of women. As chaste as Melanion,[275] we loathe the jades just as much as he did.

AN OLD MAN. You dear old woman, I would fain kiss you.

---

[275] "As chaste as Melanion" was a Greek proverb. Who Melanion was is unknown.

A WOMAN. I will set you crying without onions.

OLD MAN. ... And give you a sound kicking.

OLD WOMAN. Ah, ha! what a dense forest you have there! [*Pointing.*]

OLD MAN. So was Myronides one of the best-bearded of men o' this side; his backside was all black, and he terrified his enemies as much as Phormio.[276]

CHORUS OF WOMEN. I want to tell you a fable too, to match yours about Melanion. Once there was a certain man called Timon,[277] a tough customer, and a whimsical, a true son of the Furies, with a face that seemed to glare out of a thorn-bush. He withdrew from the world because he couldn't abide bad men, after vomiting a thousand curses at 'em. He had a holy horror of ill-conditioned fellows, but he was mighty tender towards women.

A WOMAN. Suppose I up and broke your jaw for you!

AN OLD MAN. I am not a bit afraid of you.

A WOMAN. Suppose I let fly a good kick at you?

OLD MAN. I should see your backside then.

WOMAN. You would see that, for all my age, it is very well attended to, and all fresh singed smooth.

LYSISTRATA. Ho there! come quick, come quick!

FIRST WOMAN. What is it? Why these cries?

LYSISTRATA. A man! a man! I see him approaching all afire with the flames of love. Oh! divine Queen of Cyprus, Paphos and Cythera, I pray you still be propitious to our emprise.

FIRST WOMAN. Where is he, this unknown foe?

LYSISTRATA. Yonder—beside the Temple of Demeter.

FIRST WOMAN. Yes, indeed, I see him; but who is it?

LYSISTRATA. Look, look! does any of you recognize him?

FIRST WOMAN. I do, I do! 'tis my husband Cinesias.

LYSISTRATA. To work then! Be it your task to inflame and torture and torment him. Seductions, caresses, provocations, refusals, try every means! Grant every favour,—always excepting what is forbidden by our oath on the wine-bowl.

MYRRHINÉ. Have no fear, I undertake the work.

LYSISTRATA. Well, I will stay here to help you cajole the man and set his passions aflame. The rest of you, withdraw.

CINESIAS. Alas! alas! how I am tortured by spasm and rigid convulsion! Oh! I am racked on the wheel!

LYSISTRATA. Who is this that dares to pass our lines?

CINESIAS. It is I.

LYSISTRATA. What, a man?

CINESIAS. Yes, no doubt about it, a man!

LYSISTRATA. Begone!

CINESIAS. But who are you that thus repulses me?

LYSISTRATA. The sentinel of the day.

---

[276] Myronides and Phormio were famous Athenian generals. The former was celebrated for his conquest of all Boeotia, except Thebes, in 458 B.C.; the latter, with a fleet of twenty triremes, equipped at his own cost, defeated a Lacedaemonian fleet of forty-seven sail, in 429.

[277] Timon, the misanthrope; he was an Athenian and a contemporary of Aristophanes. Disgusted by the ingratitude of his fellow-citizens and sickened with repeated disappointments, he retired altogether from society, admitting no one, it is said, to his intimacy except the brilliant young statesman Alcibiades.

CINESIAS. By all the gods, call Myrrhiné hither.

LYSISTRATA. Call Myrrhiné hither, quotha? And pray, who are you?

CINESIAS. I am her husband, Cinesias, son of Peon.

LYSISTRATA. Ah! good day, my dear friend. Your name is not unknown amongst us. Your wife has it forever on her lips; and she never touches an egg or an apple without saying: "'Twill be for Cinesias."

CINESIAS. Really and truly?

LYSISTRATA. Yes, indeed, by Aphrodité! And if we fall to talking of men, quick your wife declares: "Oh! all the rest, they're good for nothing compared with Cinesias."

CINESIAS. Oh! I beseech you, go and call her to me.

LYSISTRATA. And what will you give me for my trouble?

CINESIAS. This, if you like [*handling his tool.*] I will give you what I have there!

LYSISTRATA. Well, well, I will tell her to come.

CINESIAS. Quick, oh! be quick! Life has no more charms for me since she left my house. I am sad, sad, when I go indoors; it all seems so empty; my victuals have lost their savour. Desire is eating out my heart!

MYRRHINÉ. I love him, oh! I love him; but he won't let himself be loved. No! I shall not come.

CINESIAS. Myrrhiné, my little darling Myrrhiné, what are you saying? Come down to me quick.

MYRRHINÉ. No indeed, not I.

CINESIAS. I call you, Myrrhiné, Myrrhiné; will you not come?

MYRRHINÉ. Why should you call me? You do not want me.

CINESIAS. Not want you! Why, my weapon stands stiff with desire!

MYRRHINÉ. Good-bye.

CINESIAS. Oh! Myrrhiné, Myrrhiné, in our child's name, hear me; at any rate hear the child! Little lad, call your mother.

CHILD. Mammy, mammy, mammy!

CINESIAS. There, listen! Don't you pity the poor child? It's six days now you've never washed and never fed the child.

MYRRHINÉ. Poor darling, your father takes mighty little care of you!

CINESIAS. Come down, dearest, come down for the child's sake.

MYRRHINÉ. Ah! what a thing it is to be a mother! Well, well, we must come down, I suppose.

CINESIAS. Why, how much younger and prettier she looks! And how she looks at me so lovingly! Her cruelty and scorn only redouble my passion.

MYRRHINÉ. You are as sweet as your father is provoking! Let me kiss you, my treasure, mother's darling!

CINESIAS. Ah! what a bad thing it is to let yourself be led away by other women! Why give me such pain and suffering, and yourself into the bargain?

MYRRHINÉ. Hands off, sir!

CINESIAS. Everything is going to rack and ruin in the house.

MYRRHINÉ. I don't care.

CINESIAS. But your web that's all being pecked to pieces by the cocks and hens, don't you care for that?

MYRRHINÉ. Precious little.

CINESIAS. And Aphrodite, whose mysteries you have not celebrated for so long? Oh! won't you come back home?

MYRRHINÉ. No, at least, not till a sound Treaty put an end to the War.

CINESIAS. Well, if you wish it so much, why, we'll make it, your Treaty.

MYRRHINÉ. Well and good! When that's done, I will come home. Till then, I am bound by an oath.

CINESIAS. At any rate, let's have a short time together.

MYRRHINÉ. No, no, no! … all the same I cannot say I don't love you.

CINESIAS. You love me? Then why refuse what I ask, my little girl, my sweet Myrrhiné.

MYRRHINÉ. You must be joking! What, before the child!

CINESIAS. Manes, carry the lad home. There, you see, the child is gone; there's nothing to hinder us; let us to work!

MYRRHINÉ. But, miserable man, where, where are we to do it?

CINESIAS. In the cave of Pan; nothing could be better.

MYRRHINÉ. But how to purify myself, before going back into the citadel?

CINESIAS. Nothing easier! you can wash at the Clepsydra.[278]

MYRRHINÉ. But my oath? Do you want me to perjure myself?

CINESIAS. I take all responsibility; never make yourself anxious.

MYRRHINÉ. Well, I'll be off, then, and find a bed for us.

CINESIAS. Oh! 'tis not worth while; we can lie on the ground surely.

MYRRHINÉ. No, no! bad man as you are, I don't like your lying on the bare earth.

CINESIAS. Ah! how the dear girl loves me!

MYRRHINÉ. [coming back with a bed.] Come, get to bed quick; I am going to undress. But, plague take it, we must get a mattress.

CINESIAS. A mattress! Oh! no, never mind!

MYRRHINÉ. No, by Artemis! lie on the bare sacking, never! That were too squalid.

CINESIAS. A kiss!

MYRRHINÉ. Wait a minute!

CINESIAS. Oh! by the great gods, be quick back!

MYRRHINÉ. [coming back with a mattress.] Here is a mattress. Lie down, I am just going to undress. But, but you've got no pillow.

CINESIAS. I don't want one, no, no.

MYRRHINÉ. But I do.

CINESIAS. Oh! dear, oh, dear! they treat my poor penis for all the world like Heracles.[279]

MYRRHINÉ. [coming back with a pillow.] There, lift your head, dear!

CINESIAS. That's really everything.

MYRRHINÉ. Is it everything, I wonder.

CINESIAS. Come, my treasure.

MYRRHINÉ. I am just unfastening my girdle. But remember what you promised me about making Peace; mind you keep your word.

CINESIAS. Yes, yes, upon my life I will.

MYRRHINÉ. Why, you have no blanket.

CINESIAS. Great Zeus! what matter of that? 'tis you I want to fuck.

MYRRHINÉ. Never fear—directly, directly! I'll be back in no time.

CINESIAS. The woman will kill me with her blankets!

---

[278] A spring so named within the precincts of the Acropolis.

[279] The comic poets delighted in introducing Heracles (Hercules) on the stage as an insatiable glutton, whom the other characters were for ever tantalizing by promising toothsome dishes and then making him wait indefinitely for their arrival.

MYRRHINÉ. [*coming back with a blanket.*] Now, get up for one moment.

CINESIAS. But I tell you, our friend here is up—all stiff and ready!

MYRRHINÉ. Would you like me to scent you?

CINESIAS. No, by Apollo, no, please!

MYRRHINÉ. Yes, by Aphrodité, but I will, whether you wish it or no.

CINESIAS. Ah! great Zeus, may she soon be done!

MYRRHINÉ. [*coming back with a flask of perfume.*] Hold out your hand; now rub it in.

CINESIAS. Oh! in Apollo's name, I don't much like the smell of it; but perhaps 'twill improve when it's well rubbed in. It does not somehow smack of the marriage bed!

MYRRHINÉ. There, what a scatterbrain I am; if I have not brought Rhodian perfumes![280]

CINESIAS. Never mind, dearest, let be now.

MYRRHINÉ. You are joking!

CINESIAS. Deuce take the man who first invented perfumes, say I!

MYRRHINÉ. [*coming back with another flask.*] Here, take this bottle.

CINESIAS. I have a better all ready for your service, darling. Come, you provoking creature, to bed with you, and don't bring another thing.

MYRRHINÉ. Coming, coming; I'm just slipping off my shoes. Dear boy, will you vote for peace?

CINESIAS. I'll think about it. [*Myrrhiné runs away.*] I'm a dead man, she is killing me! She has gone, and left me in torment! I must have someone to fuck, I must! Ah me! the loveliest of women has choused and cheated me. Poor little lad (*addressing his penis*), how am I to give you what you want so badly? Where is Cynalopex? quick, man, get him a nurse, do![281]

CHORUS OF OLD MEN. Poor, miserable wretch, baulked in your amorousness! what tortures are yours! Ah! you fill me with pity. Could any man's back and loins stand such a strain? His organ stands stiff and rigid, and there's never a wench to help him!

CINESIAS. Ye gods in heaven, what pains I suffer!

CHORUS OF OLD MEN. Well, there it is; 'tis her doing, that abandoned hussy!

CINESIAS. Nay, nay! rather say that sweetest, dearest darling.

CHORUS OF OLD MEN. That dearest darling? no, no, that hussy, say I! Zeus, thou god of the skies, canst not let loose a hurricane, to sweep them all up into the air, and whirl 'em round, then drop 'em down crash! and impale them on the point of his weapon!

A HERALD. Say, where shall I find the Senate and the Prytanes? I am bearer of despatches.

MAGISTRATE. But are you a man or a Priapus, pray?[282]

HERALD. Oh! but he's mighty simple. I am a herald, of course, I swear I am, and I come from Sparta about making peace.

MAGISTRATE. But look, you are hiding a lance under your clothes, surely.

HERALD. No, nothing of the sort.

MAGISTRATE. Then why do you turn away like that, and hold your cloak out from your body? Have you gotten swellings in the groin with your journey?

HERALD. By the twin brethren! the man's an old maniac.

MAGISTRATE. Ah, ha! my fine lad, why I can see it standing, oh fie!

---

[280] The Rhodian perfumes and unguents were less esteemed than the Syrian.

[281] 'Dog-fox,' nickname of a certain notorious Philostratus, keeper of an Athenian brothel of note in Aristophanes' day.

[282] The god of gardens—and of lubricity; represented by a grotesque figure with an enormous penis.

HERALD. I tell you no! but enough of this foolery.

MAGISTRATE. Well, what is it you have there then?

HERALD. A Lacedaemonian 'skytalé.'[283]

MAGISTRATE. Oh, indeed, a 'skytalé,' is it? Well, well, speak out frankly; I know all about these matters. How are things going at Sparta now?

HERALD. Why, everything is turned upside down at Sparta; and all the allies are half dead with lusting. We simply must have Pellené.[284]

MAGISTRATE. What is the reason of it all? Is it the god Pan's doing?

HERALD. No, but Lampito's and the Spartan women's, acting at her instigation; they have denied the men all access to their cunts.

MAGISTRATE. But whatever do you do?

HERALD. We are at our wits' end; we walk bent double, just as if we were carrying lanterns in a wind. The jades have sworn we shall not so much as touch their cunts till we have all agreed to conclude peace.

MAGISTRATE. Ha, ha! So I see now, 'tis a general conspiracy embracing all Greece. Go you back to Sparta and bid them send Envoys with plenary powers to treat for peace. I will urge our Senators myself to name Plenipotentiaries from us; and to persuade them, why, I will show them this. [*Pointing to his erect penis.*]

HERALD. What could be better? I fly at your command.

CHORUS OF OLD MEN. No wild beast is there, no flame of fire, more fierce and untameable than woman; the panther is less savage and shameless.

CHORUS OF WOMEN. And yet you dare to make war upon me, wretch, when you might have me for your most faithful friend and ally.

CHORUS OF OLD MEN. Never, never can my hatred cease towards women.

CHORUS OF WOMEN. Well, please yourself. Still I cannot bear to leave you all naked as you are; folks would laugh at me. Come, I am going to put this tunic on you.

CHORUS OF OLD MEN. You are right, upon my word! it was only in my confounded fit of rage I took it off.

CHORUS OF WOMEN. Now at any rate you look like a man, and they won't make fun of you. Ah! if you had not offended me so badly, I would take out that nasty insect you have in your eye for you.

CHORUS OF OLD MEN. Ah! so that's what was annoying me so! Look, here's a ring, just remove the insect, and show it me. By Zeus! it has been hurting my eye this ever so long.

CHORUS OF WOMEN. Well, I agree, though your manners are not over and above pleasant. Oh! what a huge great gnat! just look! It's from Tricorysus, for sure.[285]

CHORUS OF OLD MEN. A thousand thanks! the creature was digging a regular well in my eye; now it's gone, my tears flow freely.

CHORUS OF WOMEN. I will wipe them for you—bad, naughty man though you are. Now, just one kiss.

CHORUS OF OLD MEN. No—a kiss, certainly not!

---

[283] A staff in use among the Lacedaemonians for writing cipher despatches. A strip of leather or paper was wound round the 'skytalé,' on which the required message was written lengthwise, so that when unrolled it became unintelligible; the recipient abroad had a staff of the same thickness and pattern, and so was enabled by rewinding the document to decipher the words.

[284] A city of Achaia, the acquisition of which had long been an object of Lacedaemonian ambition. To make the joke intelligible here, we must suppose Pellené was also the name of some notorious courtesan of the day.

[285] A deme of Attica, abounding in woods and marshes, where the gnats were particularly troublesome. There is very likely also an allusion to the spiteful, teasing character of its inhabitants.

CHORUS OF WOMEN. Just one, whether you like it or not.

CHORUS OF OLD MEN. Oh! those confounded women! how they do cajole us! How true the saying: "'Tis impossible to live with the baggages, impossible to live without 'em"! Come, let us agree for the future not to regard each other any more as enemies; and to clinch the bargain, let us sing a choric song.

CHORUS OF WOMEN. We desire, Athenians, to speak ill of no man; but on the contrary to say much good of everyone, and to *do* the like. We have had enough of misfortunes and calamities. Is there any, man or woman, wants a bit of money—two or three minas or so;[286] well, our purse is full. If only peace is concluded, the borrower will not have to pay back. Also I'm inviting to supper a few Carystian friends,[287] who are excellently well qualified. I have still a drop of good soup left, and a young porker I'm going to kill, and the flesh will be sweet and tender. I shall expect you at my house to-day; but first away to the baths with you, you and your children; then come all of you, ask no one's leave, but walk straight up, as if you were at home; never fear, the door will be ... shut in your faces![288]

CHORUS OF OLD MEN. Ah! here come the Envoys from Sparta with their long flowing beards; why, you would think they wore a cage[289] between their thighs. [*Enter the Lacedaemonian Envoys.*] Hail to you, first of all, Laconians; then tell us how you fare.

A LACONIAN. No need for many words; you see what a state we are in.

CHORUS OF OLD MEN. Alas! the situation grows more and more strained! the intensity of the thing is just frightful.

LACONIAN. 'Tis beyond belief. But to work! summon your Commissioners, and let us patch up the best peace we may.

CHORUS OF OLD MEN. Ah! our men too, like wrestlers in the arena, cannot endure a rag over their bellies; 'tis an athlete's malady, which only exercise can remedy.

AN ATHENIAN. Can anybody tell us where Lysistrata is? Surely she will have some compassion on our condition.

CHORUS OF OLD MEN. Look! 'tis the very same complaint. [*Addressing the Athenian.*] Don't you feel of mornings a strong nervous tension?

ATHENIAN. Yes, and a dreadful, dreadful torture it is! Unless peace is made very soon, we shall find no resource but to fuck Clisthenes.[290]

CHORUS OF OLD MEN. Take my advice, and put on your clothes again; one of the fellows who mutilated the Hermae[291] might see you.

ATHENIAN. You are right.

LACONIAN. Quite right. There, I will slip on my tunic.

ATHENIAN. Oh! what a terrible state we are in! Greeting to you, Laconian fellow-sufferers.

---

[286] A mina was a little over £4; 60 minas made a talent.

[287] Carystus was a city of Euboea notorious for the dissoluteness of its inhabitants; hence the inclusion of these Carystian youths in the women's invitation.

[288] A [Greek: para prosdokian]; *i.e.* exactly the opposite of the word expected is used to conclude the sentence—to move the sudden hilarity of the audience as a finale to the scene.

[289] A wattled cage or pen for pigs.

[290] An effeminate, a pathic; failing women, they will have to resort to pederasty.

[291] These *Hermae* were half-length figures of the god Hermes, which stood at the corners of streets and in public places at Athens. One night, just before the sailing of the Sicilian Expedition, they were all mutilated—to the consternation of the inhabitants. Alcibiades and his wild companions were suspected of the outrage.

LACONIAN. [*addressing one of his countrymen.*] Ah! my boy, what a thing it would have been if these fellows had seen us just now when our tools were on full stand!

ATHENIAN. Speak out, Laconians, what is it brings you here?

LACONIAN. We have come to treat for peace.

ATHENIAN. Well said; we are of the same mind. Better call Lysistrata then; she is the only person will bring us to terms.

LACONIAN. Yes, yes—and Lysistratus into the bargain, if you will.

CHORUS OF OLD MEN. Needless to call her; she has heard your voices, and here she comes.

ATHENIAN. Hail, boldest and bravest of womankind! The time is come to show yourself in turn uncompromising and conciliatory, exacting and yielding, haughty and condescending. Call up all your skill and artfulness. Lo! the foremost men in Hellas, seduced by your fascinations, are agreed to entrust you with the task of ending their quarrels.

LYSISTRATA. 'Twill be an easy task—if only they refrain from mutual indulgence in masculine love; if they do, I shall know the fact at once. Now, where is the gentle goddess Peace? Lead hither the Laconian Envoys. But, look you, no roughness or violence; our husbands always behaved so boorishly.[292] Bring them to me with smiles, as women should. If any refuse to give you his hand, then catch him by the penis and draw him politely forward. Bring up the Athenians too; you may take them just how you will. Laconians, approach; and you, Athenians, on my other side. Now hearken all! I am but a woman; but I have good common sense; Nature has dowered me with discriminating judgment, which I have yet further developed, thanks to the wise teachings of my father and the elders of the city. First I must bring a reproach against you that applies equally to both sides. At Olympia, and Thermopylae, and Delphi, and a score of other places too numerous to mention, you celebrate before the same altars ceremonies common to all Hellenes; yet you go cutting each other's throats, and sacking Hellenic cities, when all the while the Barbarian is yonder threatening you! That is my first point.

ATHENIAN. Ah, ah! concupiscence is killing me!

LYSISTRATA. Now 'tis to you I address myself, Laconians. Have you forgotten how Periclides,[293] your own countryman, sat a suppliant before our altars? How pale he was in his purple robes! He had come to crave an army of us; 'twas the time when Messenia was pressing you sore, and the Sea-god was shaking the earth. Cimon marched to your aid at the head of four thousand hoplites, and saved Lacedaemon. And, after such a service as that, you ravage the soil of your benefactors!

ATHENIAN. They do wrong, very wrong, Lysistrata.

LACONIAN. We do wrong, very wrong. Ah! great gods! what lovely thighs she has!

LYSISTRATA. And now a word to the Athenians. Have you no memory left of how, in the days when ye wore the tunic of slaves, the Laconians came, spear in hand, and slew a host of Thessalians and partisans of Hippias the Tyrant? They, and they only, fought on your side on that eventful day; they delivered you from despotism, and

---

[292] They had repeatedly dismissed with scant courtesy successive Lacedaemonian embassies coming to propose terms of peace after the notable Athenian successes at Pylos, when the Island of Sphacteria was captured and 600 Spartan citizens brought prisoners to Athens. This was in 425 B.C., the seventh year of the War.

[293] Chief of the Lacedaemonian embassy which came to Athens, after the earthquake of 464 B.C., which almost annihilated the town of Sparta, to invoke the help of the Athenians against the revolted Messenians and helots.

thanks to them our Nation could change the short tunic of the slave for the long cloak of the free man.

LACONIAN. I have never seen a woman of more gracious dignity.

ATHENIAN. I have never seen a woman with a finer cunt!

LYSISTRATA. Bound by such ties of mutual kindness, how can you bear to be at war? Stop, stay the hateful strife, be reconciled; what hinders you?

LACONIAN. We are quite ready, if they will give us back our rampart.

LYSISTRATA. What rampart, my dear man?

LACONIAN. Pylos, which we have been asking for and craving for ever so long.

ATHENIAN. In the Sea-god's name, you shall never have it!

LYSISTRATA. Agree, my friends, agree.

ATHENIAN. But then what city shall we be able to stir up trouble in?

LYSISTRATA. Ask for another place in exchange.

ATHENIAN. Ah! that's the ticket! Well, to begin with, give us Echinus, the Maliac gulf adjoining, and the two legs of Megara.[294]

LACONIAN. Oh! surely, surely not all that, my dear sir.

LYSISTRATA. Come to terms; never make a difficulty of two legs more or less!

ATHENIAN. Well, I'm ready now to off coat and cultivate my land.

LACONIAN. And I too, to dung it to start with.

LYSISTRATA. That's just what you shall do, once peace is signed. So, if you really want to make it, go consult your allies about the matter.

ATHENIAN. What allies, I should like to know? Why, we are *all* on the stand; not one but is mad to be fucking. What we all want, is to be abed with our wives; how should our allies fail to second our project?

LACONIAN. And ours the same, for certain sure!

ATHENIANS. The Carystians first and foremost, by the gods!

LYSISTRATA. Well said, indeed! Now be off to purify yourselves for entering the Acropolis, where the women invite you to supper; we will empty our provision baskets to do you honour. At table, you will exchange oaths and pledges; then each man will go home with his wife.

ATHENIAN. Come along then, and as quick as may be.

LACONIAN. Lead on; I'm your man.

ATHENIAN. Quick, quick's the word, say I.

CHORUS OF WOMEN. Embroidered stuffs, and dainty tunics, and flowing gowns, and golden ornaments, everything I have, I offer them you with all my heart; take them all for your children, for your girls, against they are chosen "basket-bearers" to the goddess. I invite you every one to enter, come in and choose whatever you will; there is nothing so well fastened, you cannot break the seals, and carry away the contents. Look about you everywhere ... you won't find a blessed thing, unless you have sharper eyes than mine.[295] And if any of you lacks corn to feed his slaves and his young and numerous family, why, I have a few grains of wheat at home; let him take what I have to give, a big twelve-pound loaf included. So let my poorer neighbours

---

[294] Echinus was a town on the Thessalian coast, at the entrance to the Maliac Gulf, near Thermopylae and opposite the northern end of the Athenian island of Euboea. By the "legs of Megara" are meant the two "long walls" or lines of fortification connecting the city of Megara with its seaport Nisaea—in the same way as Piraeus was joined to Athens.

[295] Examples of [Greek: para prosdokian] again; see above.

all come with bags and wallets; my man, Manes, shall give them corn; but I warn them not to come near my door, or—beware the dog![296]

A MARKET-LOUNGER. I say, you, open the door!

A SLAVE. Go your way, I tell you. Why, bless me, they're sitting down now; I shall have to singe 'em with my torch to make 'em stir! What an impudent lot of fellows!

MARKET-LOUNGER. I don't mean to budge.

SLAVE. Well, as you *must* stop, and I don't want to offend you—but you'll see some queer sights.

MARKET-LOUNGER. Well and good, I've no objection.

SLAVE. No, no, you must be off—or I'll tear your hair out, I will; be off, I say, and don't annoy the Laconian Envoys; they're just coming out from the banquet-hall.

AN ATHENIAN. Such a merry banquet I've never seen before! The Laconians were simply charming. After the drink is in, why, we're all wise men, all. It's only natural, to be sure, for sober, we're all fools. Take my advice, my fellow-countrymen, our Envoys should always be drunk. We go to Sparta; we enter the city sober; why, we must be picking a quarrel directly. We don't understand what they say to us, we imagine a lot they don't say at all, and we report home all wrong, all topsy-turvy. But, look you, to-day it's quite different; we're enchanted whatever happens; instead of Clitagoras, they might sing us Telamon,[297] and we should clap our hands just the same. A perjury or two into the bargain, la! what does that matter to merry companions in their cups?

SLAVE. But here they are back again! Will you begone, you loafing scoundrels.

MARKET-LOUNGER. Ah ha! here's the company coming out already.

A LACONIAN. My dear, sweet friend, come, take your flute in hand; I would fain dance and sing my best in honour of the Athenians and our noble selves.

AN ATHENIAN. Yes, take your flute, i' the gods' name. What a delight to see him dance!

CHORUS OF LACONIANS. Oh Mnemosyné! inspire these men, inspire my muse who knows our exploits and those of the Athenians. With what a godlike ardour did they swoop down at Artemisium[298] on the ships of the Medes! What a glorious victory was that! For the soldiers of Leonidas,[299] they were like fierce wild-boars whetting their tushes. The sweat ran down their faces, and drenched all their limbs, for verily the Persians were as many as the sands of the seashore. Oh! Artemis, huntress queen, whose arrows pierce the denizens of the woods, virgin goddess, be thou favourable to the Peace we here conclude; through thee may our hearts be long united! May this treaty draw close for ever the bonds of a happy friendship! No more wiles and stratagems! Aid us, oh! aid us, maiden huntress!

LYSISTRATA. All is for the best; and now, Laconians, take your wives away home with you, and you, Athenians, yours. May husband live happily with wife, and wife with husband. Dance, dance, to celebrate our bliss, and let us be heedful to avoid like mistakes for the future.

CHORUS OF ATHENIANS Appear, appear, dancers, and the Graces with you! Let us invoke, one and all, Artemis, and her heavenly brother, gracious Apollo, patron of

---

[296] Examples of [Greek: para prosdokian] again; see above.

[297] Clitagoras was a composer of drinking songs, Telamon of war songs.

[298] Here, off the north coast of Euboea, the Greeks defeated the Persians in a naval battle, 480 B.C.

[299] The hero of Thermopylae, where the 300 Athenians arrested the advance of the invading hosts of Xerxes in the same year.

the dance, and Dionysus, whose eye darts flame, as he steps forward surrounded by the Maenad maids, and Zeus, who wields the flashing lightning, and his august, thrice-blessed spouse, the Queen of Heaven! These let us invoke, and all the other gods, calling all the inhabitants of the skies to witness the noble Peace now concluded under the fond auspices of Aphrodité. Io Paean! Io Paean! dance, leap, as in honour of a victory won. Evoé! Evoé! And you, our Laconian guests, sing us a new and inspiring strain!

CHORUS OF LACONIANS. Leave once more, oh! leave once more the noble height of Taygetus, oh! Muse of Lacedaemon, and join us in singing the praises of Apollo of Amyclae, and Athena of the Brazen House, and the gallant twin sons of Tyndarus, who practise arms on the banks of Eurotas river.[300] Haste, haste hither with nimble-footed pace, let us sing Sparta, the city that delights in choruses divinely sweet and graceful dances, when our maidens bound lightly by the river side, like frolicsome fillies, beating the ground with rapid steps and shaking their long locks in the wind, as Bacchantes wave their wands in the wild revels of the Wine-god. At their head, oh! chaste and beauteous goddess, daughter of Latona, Artemis, do thou lead the song and dance. A fillet binding thy waving tresses, appear in thy loveliness; leap like a fawn; strike thy divine hands together to animate the dance, and aid us to renown the valiant goddess of battles, great Athené of the Brazen House!

---

[300] Amyclae, an ancient town on the Eurotas within two or three miles of Sparta, the traditional birthplace of Castor and Pollux; here stood a famous and magnificent Temple of Apollo.

"Of the Brazen House," a surname of Athené, from the Temple dedicated to her worship at Chalcis in Euboea, the walls of which were covered with plates of brass.

Sons of Tyndarus, that is, Castor and Pollux, "the great twin brethren," held in peculiar reverence at Sparta.

CPSIA information can be obtained at www.ICGtesting.com
Printed in the USA
LVOW08s0010200716

496999LV00002B/192/P